ALTARS to THRONES

Uncovering the Mystery of Unanswered Prayer

DR. PETER BONADIE

ALTARS TO THRONES — Uncovering The Mystery of Unanswered Prayer

Copyright © 2018 by Dr. Peter Bonadie

Printed in the United States of America

ISBN 978-0-9991381-3-7 (Paperback)

All rights reserved solely by the author. The author guarantees all contents are original and do not infringe upon the legal rights of any other person or work. No part of this book may be reproduced, stored in a retrieval system, or transmitted in any form or by any means without expressed written permission of the author.

All quotes, unless otherwise noted, are from the HOLY BIBLE, NEW INTERNATIONAL VERSION (NIV). Copyright © 1973, 1978, 1984 by International Bible Society. Used by permission of Zondervan Publishing House. All rights reserved.

Scriptures marked KJV are taken from The Holy Bible, King James Version. Copyright © 1972 by Thomas Nelson Inc., Camden, New Jersey 08103.

Scriptures marked AMP are taken from The Amplified Bible, containing the amplified Old Testament and the Amplified New Testament. 1987. The Lockman Foundation: La Habra, CA.

Scriptures marked AMPC are taken from The Amplified Bible, Classic Edition, Copyright © 1954, 1958, 1962, 1964, 1965, 1987. The Lockman Foundation: La Habra, CA.

Scriptures marked NKJV are from the New King James Version. Copyright 1979, 1980, 1982 by Thomas Nelson, Inc. Used by permission. All rights reserved.

Scriptures marked TLB are taken from The Living Bible. Copyright © 1971 by Tyndale House Publishers, Wheaton, Illinois 60187. All rights reserved.

Scriptures marked NASB are taken from the New American Standard Bible. Copyright © 1960, 1962, 1963, 1968, 1971, 1972, 1973, 1975, 1977, 1995 by The Lockman Foundation. All rights reserved.

Scriptures marked MSG are taken from The Message Bible. Published by permission. Originally published by NavPress in English as THE MESSAGE: The Bible in Contemporary Language copyright 2002 by Eugene Peterson. All rights reserved. (The Message Bible Online)

Scriptures marked CSB are taken from The Christian Standard Bible. Copyright © 2017 by Holman Bible Publishers. All rights reserved.

Scriptures marked MEV are from The Holy Bible, Modern English Version. Copyright © 2014 by Military Bible Association. Published and distributed by Charisma House. All rights reserved.

Scriptures marked EHV are from the Evangelical Heritage Version of the Bible, New Testament & Psalms ©2017. All rights reserved.

Published by:
Peter Bonadie Ministries Inc.
770 Park Place
Brooklyn, NY 11216
Tel: 347-281-9059
Email: apostlebonadie@gmail.com
www.peterbonadieministries.org

Editing & Layout by:
Marlon Nicolls & Associates
www.marlonicolls.com
USA: 347-459-4027

Cover Design by:
Sheldon Elliott
info@pixelstudionyc.com

DEDICATION

This book is dedicated to the intercessors who serve at the phones at Kingdom Life Ministries. I dedicate it to them in gratitude for the long hours of sacrifice and willingness to serve the people of God. They have labored tirelessly, fighting the weariness of the body and the urgent demand for sleep. Whereas I cannot call all the names, there are some who stand out in an amazing way. They have prayed thousands of prayers in the early hours of the morning and have been an invaluable source of faith and hope for thousands.

ACKNOWLEDGEMENTS

I wish to acknowledge Apostle John Eckhardt who has inspired me to write this book. We spoke many times on the phone, and though he may not be aware of it, he made me realize that I *do* have something to tell the world.

Then I want to remember my dear and precious wife, Shelly-Ann, who allows me, without fuss, to follow hard after the things of God. She is an amazing woman. I love and thank you for your trust and confidence.

TESTIMONIALS

Having been a pastor for all of my adult life, I have seen the progression of favorable responses to my prayer as I learnt to approach God correctly. As a result of the knowledge acquired, we currently run a powerful prayer system in Brooklyn, New York, and host a daily radio program that brings thousands together to pray. Our prayer lines are sometimes flooded with people seeking for the help that God alone can give. The principles shared in this book have proven to be very effective and powerful, and have produced some amazing results. Just to name a few:

1. A lady testified that she was healed of AIDS after living with the virus for seven years.

2. Another woman walked into our church and told the story of how we prayed for her and the doctors were baffled at her amazing recovery; having been a person who moved from stage four cancer to being totally cancer-free.

3. One day as I entered our church, a woman came and lifted me up. I was very concerned about this unusual action by a complete stranger, but she eventually put me down and proceeded to tell me why she had reacted that way. Her grandmother had fallen down, hitting her head, and was rushed to the hospital in critical

condition. They declared her clinically dead by the time the doctors got to her. This lady said that she called my prayer line and we prayed a simple but powerful prayer. The grandmother lived! Glory to God! When I heard that powerful testimony, I shouted, "Lift me up again!!!"

4. One family had lost contact with a brother for over 21 years. No one knew where he was. Many in the family thought that he was dead. They brought the problem to our team. We prayed that Sunday, and by the Monday, the brother called. He said that he just suddenly had an unusual urge to contact his family.

5. A faithful member of our church got ill with a heart condition. When I heard about it, I called and spoke to them while they were in the emergency room. I instructed her numbers to normalize, as at that moment they were running wild. While praying, I heard her husband exclaim, because he literally witnessed the numbers fall to normal readings. The nurse came to the room and checked all the cables because they could not explain how a condition could change so quickly.

6. One immigrant came to me with a deep personal cry to have her status regularized. I prayed with her. In a matter of weeks, the Green-Card was in the mail.

7.   We have seen numerous barren wombs opened and children coming forth, healthy and strong.

Over and over again we see the handiwork of God in powerful release. There have been many signs and wonders. There have been angelic visitations time and time again. There are those who have come to us and said that Kingdom Life Ministries International is the best kept secret in the city. Hundreds of thousands of people have called looking for the help that God alone can give; and have received from the hand of the Lord.

CONTENTS

Dedication

Acknowledgements

Testimonials

Foreword ii

Introduction vi

1. The Mystery of Unanswered Prayer 1

2. Altars – Our Passage to His Presence 31

3. Beyond the Altars 55

4. Holding On To the Horns of the Altar 77

5. Altars – Foundations for Effective Prayer 105

6. Principles for Effective Prayer 135

7. We are God's Legislative Executive 165

8. Rulers of the Material World 193

9. Intercessors In The Throne 221

FOREWORD

The book in your hand, ***"Altars to Thrones"***, bears uncommon insights into the deep things of God regarding 'Prayer'. It deals with the mystery of unanswered prayer from a powerful angle. It will administer a new righteous resolve and inspiration to pray like never before.

Apostle Peter Bonadie has been my friend for many years and I have had the privilege of sharing pulpits with him in many different countries, on diverse continents across the globe. We both served and ministered in South Africa, USA, The Netherlands, The Caribbean and India. Apostle Peter's brilliant mind is an undeniable attribute that has been a source of wealth for many who have met him and have been on the receiving end of his ministry.

In my experience of connecting with hundreds of key Apostolic voices that are movers and shakers, shifting spiritual climates, and witnessing the demonstration of the power of God, I have come to recognize that effective prayer is a key to any significant work of God. Revivals, Spiritual Awakenings and Reformations are ignited and sustained by prayer. This book enters the arena of other great writings and contributes to the economy of intercession. I am personally impressed with its content.

"Altars to Thrones" begins with a somewhat humorous but sobering analysis of the problem of unanswered prayer. This subject was of great interest to me, as I, too, have had many of my prayers go unanswered in the past, and was thrilled to discover the solution to this puzzling complication.

Rather than attributing effective prayer into a series of steps and then analysing failure in terms of missing some steps, Dr. Bonadie points to two major issues. Firstly, he points to issues of the 'content' of prayer and the 'internal posturing' of the intercessor. These are new and profound ways of looking at the mystery of unanswered prayer.

I am further impressed with the concepts he gleaned from studies on the Altar Factors in the Old Testament. I also admire the depth of revelation he extracted from the writings of the patriarchs and the prophets. While not destroying the Old order, he skilfully builds upon it until he showed how the New Testament does not carry much revelation on Altars, but rather, it shows the Church—the Bride of Christ—seated in heavenly realms in the Throne Room of God. This is a new and superb concept. The reader and believer, I am confident, would become a much more effective intercessor once this view is grasped.

There is a solid theological framework seen in the life-giving dissemination of the revelation displayed in this book. It is a gem!!! There is the touch of God that has been transmitted from Apostle Peter's life into the very penned words you are about to read.

Every chapter is chock-full with revelatory insight that will mature the reader into becoming a more accurate, effective intercessor. You will discover how to exclude "unanswered" prayers from your life and see greater results on a more consistent basis.

I have found the last chapter to be extremely exhilarating reading. One has to approach this chapter almost like on tippy toe. It takes the reader into the Throne Room of God and places the Church into a Global Tribunal (as he calls it)—the Supreme Court of the Universe. It is there that the saints will execute the written judgements of God on wicked nations and evil systems. It is there that one will see how not to beg as orphans and paupers, but to legislate as Kings. The vast content in this simple book is as a child playing on the edge of an ocean in water gently flowing back and forth. Yet that ocean is vast and deep.

I encourage every reader to take this life-altering journey and move from prayerlessness to prayerfulness; from ineffectiveness to effectiveness; from begging to legislating. You are sure to undergo a transformation in your thinking to such an extent, that you will cease from acting like peasants in a field and begin reigning like royalty in a palace.

—Dr. Romero Maridjan
  Doctorate in Ministry
  Founder of RSM Ministries
  CEO of Dominion Training Institute
  The Netherlands

INTRODUCTION

Unanswered prayer has been a baffling mystery for many of God's people over the years. I have seen countless Christians become frustrated because most of their prayers are seemingly left hanging without an answer from God. They pray, but have not yet come to the realization that 'effective prayer' is an art. This book takes the reader on an exciting journey to help resolve this puzzling enigma; and is ideal to be used as a manual for many aspiring intercessors.

One of the key components shared in this book is derived from the fact that the 'Old Testament' provides us with a revelation that bases the force of prayer around the dynamics or the purposes of the Altar, and of people looking 'upward' to God. What is also amplified is the revelation that the Church ought to pray from the place of the **Throne**. From this position, the people of God are not just directing their prayers 'upward' to God, but also legislating 'downward' to the material world, the events of history, and against Satan and his band of cohorts. It is noticeable that the 'New Testament' does not emphasize the revelation of 'Altars'; it focuses more of its attention on the revelation of 'Thrones'. It is my belief that the mystery of unanswered prayer is hidden in this area.

We are often asking God *for* things He has already given to us. We also ask Him to *do* things that He already told *us* to do. We should not ask Him to make disciples. That prayer will **never** be answered, because He told us to **"Go and make disciples…"**

We will discover a new and improved way to move in the realm of God and obtain swifter responses from Heaven. When applied, the principles taught in this book would produce amazing encounters with God and greater manifestations of the Father.

Read this book prayerfully and seek to understand it. It can be the game changer that you have been praying for.

> "If all the prayers in the world were answered, there would be a global Utopia."

CHAPTER 1

The Mystery of Unanswered Prayer

If all the prayers in the world were answered, there would be a global Utopia. First of all, let us consider that there are about 1.3 billion Christians in the world today; over a billion Muslims; millions of Buddhists, Hindus, and Judaizes; and all of these religions hold prayer as a central practice of their faith. Each of these religions, for the most part, pray for goodwill, prosperity, peace and longevity.

If we assume that Muslims pray faithfully, there would be at least three billion prayers daily; and if Christians do so as well, you can easily add about another billion. Christians sometimes, especially charismatics, bind demons, cast them to hell, pray for them to cease and desist from their evil works. If we add those prayers to the petitions of all the other major world religions, we can conclude that at least **ten billion** prayers go up to Heaven daily.

When we factor in the numerous prayer-meetings, fasting, watchings, prayer conferences and so on, that number would probably quadruple. If these prayers were answered, there would be no demon on the earth, not one sick nor poor. The world would be in perfect peace. Our governmental and legal systems would have justice for all. One look at the world around us, however, would reveal a mysterious contradiction.

Worsening this apparent impenetrable mystery, is the fact that these prayers are prayed by some of the most supposedly faithful, righteous and anointed people on earth. We have priests, pundits, pastors, prophets, apostles, evangelists, teachers, deacons, elders, popes, great miracle workers, and most holy people praying. These prayers are customarily uttered with white robes, raised voices, weeping hearts, or victorious shouts.

Yet, despite all the vigor and maneuvers exerted during this vital discipline, I have noticed a stark 'ineffectiveness' when it comes to getting answers to our prayer. Wars, and the threat of wars disturb the peace and negatively affect financial markets. Additionally, storm after storm create instability and destruction to human lives and topple economies in an instant. Earthquakes, tsunamis, hurricanes, volcanic eruptions, tornadoes and floods come with such sovereign powers, defying modern science and technology's ability to restrain them.

Hundreds of millions still live in abject poverty notwithstanding all the prayers that go up for all such people.

THE MYSTERY OF UNANSWERED PRAYER

I was in Chennai, India, with my friend Dr. Manicham Prakash, where I saw people who were born and lived on the side-walk. Poor environmental conditions are the permanent state in which they live. Such inadequate sanitation almost always exists with substandard housing. Because the poor in developing nations commonly have little or no running water or sewage facilities, human excrement and garbage accumulate, quickly becoming a breeding ground for disease. In cities, especially in ghettoes and shantytowns that house the very poor, overcrowding can lead to high transmission rates of infectious and airborne diseases. The poor are also often uneducated or miseducated about the spread of diseases, making them extremely vulnerable to death and destruction. It will appear that despite the billions of daily prayers, it is baffling that the negative socio-economic and political conditions sustain. It has become quite clear to me that we, as 'pray-ers', are yet to unravel the secret to praying effective, impactful prayers.

On a personal level, I have had some very humorous experiences with regards to prayer in the past. When I came to know the Lord, fortunately for me, one of the first emphases I learnt in classic Pentecostalism is that you must have a prayer life. So, I prayed without ceasing. I fasted as often as I could, sometimes for days, and I was only sixteen years old at the time. I sacrificially fasted on my birthdays and special holidays such as Christmas, to demonstrate to the Lord how serious I was about prayer. It was my attempt to beat the flesh into subjection. I prayed long and hard. Sometimes I stayed up all night in what we used to call 'watchings'. Those were days of simplicity and sincerity of heart. They were good days and some great things happened, which cannot be denied. Yet, if **all** that I had prayed for had actually materialized in my life, I would have a worldwide ministry by now, innumerable members in my church, and millions of dollars in my possession. I guess I do not have to tell you that none of those have happened. You should be smiling and identifying with this experience.

Some of my experiences would make you laugh hysterically. Early in the days of my walk with the Lord, I was part of a group of seven men that we called Deliverance Ministry. We learnt from the Word of God that we could lay hands of the sick and see them recover (Mark 16:18). We excitedly ran off to pray for a crippled woman in her home where she had been bedridden for years. We were boldly determined that she would walk again. After we had prayed loudly and intensely for about an hour or so, I reached out, remembering what the Apostle Peter did to the crippled man at the Temple Gate-and pulled the lady off the bed. She fell to the ground with a loud "THUD!" Regrettably, she did not walk at all. Word was spread abroad in the town that, "Peter had killed this 'Mrs. So-and-So' in prayer."

It wasn't long after that, we proceeded to pray for another lady in the community. This one was a dear and precious schoolmate of mine. She had fallen ill with leukemia and was given up by the doctors to die. Again, with a new and undaunted faith, I proceeded to pray for her with youthful zeal. Before going to see her, I was warned that she was no longer the beautiful lady I once knew. I was not prepared for what I saw. Her appearance really was unusual as the cancer had sucked the physical beauty out of her. I laid hands on her and shook her violently hoping for a genuine transfer of the **'healing anointing'**. Unfortunately, there was no such transference. Days later she died. Now, word was out all over the town again, "Do not let Brother Peter pray for you, because death most certainly follows!"

Often, church folk celebrate negligible and questionable answers to prayer. Shouts of joy usually erupt when someone's knee is not paining them anymore, or if a headache or some minor ailment is healed. I am in no way minimizing the power of God that is released to graciously bring relief into a recipient's life, but rather, my intent is to point to the 'moderate' level of miraculous happenings that the Church, for the most part, has been experiencing.

Once a man of God came to my church and celebrated how God answered his prayer by causing him to find some money in his pocket. So, there was a time I needed some money and found some in a pants that I wore and hung in my closet. As I raised my voice to give thanks to God for putting it there, the Lord rebuked me and said that it was a manifestation of my carelessness and lack of fiscal discipline that the money was left there. But it is that kind of answer to prayer that we have become used to.

When have we seen missing limbs grow back as a consequence of our prayers? When last have we seen someone raised from the dead? When was the last time we saw teleportation? When have we ever witnessed someone speak against a tornado or hurricane and turn it back? When last did we see someone move the elements or change the molecular structure of an object, such as turning water into wine? In fact, have we EVER seen such noteworthy happenings???!!! In Jerusalem, outstanding miracles were observed with awe, as was recorded in Acts 4:15-16:

> *^{15} But when they had commanded them to go aside out of the council, they conferred among themselves, ^{16} Saying, What shall we do to these men? for that indeed a **notable miracle** hath been done by them is manifest to all them that dwell in Jerusalem;* **and we cannot deny it.** (KJV - Emphasis Added)

Here we see a ***notable miracle*** done amongst the people and it was undeniable. Oh, that God would revive His work in our time and communities!

God is said to have done extraordinary deeds through many of His servants. In Acts 19:11-12 it is documented that:

> ^{11} **God did extraordinary miracles through Paul**, *^{12} so that even handkerchiefs and aprons that had touched him were taken to the sick, and their illnesses were cured and the evil spirits left them.* (NIV - Emphasis Added)

Where is the God of Elijah? Where is the God of signs and wonders? You must admit, something is wrong, or we just have not gotten it right at all. We must be missing something here. Consider these awe-inspiring manifestations of God:

THE MYSTERY OF UNANSWERED PRAYER

1. A Little Boy's Lunch Fed Thousands

^{17} "We have here only five loaves of bread and two fish," they answered. ^{18} "Bring them here to me," he said. ^{19} And he directed the people to sit down on the grass. Taking the five loaves and the two fish and looking up to heaven, he gave thanks and broke the loaves. Then he gave them to the disciples, and the disciples gave them to the people. ^{20} They all ate and were satisfied, and the disciples picked up twelve basketfuls of broken pieces that were left over. ^{21} The number of those who ate was about five thousand men, besides women and children. (Matthew 14:17-21 - NIV)

2. The Red Sea Parted

^{21} Then Moses stretched out his hand over the sea, and all that night the Lord drove the sea back with a strong east wind and turned it into dry land. The waters were divided, ^{22} and the Israelites went through the sea on dry ground, with a wall of water on their right and on their left. (Exodus 14:21-22 - NIV)

3. A River Parted

^{14} So when the people broke camp to cross the Jordan, the priests carrying the ark of the covenant went ahead of them. ^{15} Now the Jordan is at flood stage all during harvest. Yet as soon as the priests who carried the ark reached the Jordan and their feet touched the water's

edge, ¹⁶ *the water from upstream stopped flowing. It piled up in a heap a great distance away, at a town called Adam in the vicinity of Zarethan, while the water flowing down to the Sea of the Arabah (that is, the Dead Sea) was completely cut off. So the people crossed over opposite Jericho.* (Joshua 3:14-16 - NIV)

4. Shadow Moved in the Opposite Direction

⁷ "'This is the Lord's sign to you that the Lord will do what he has promised: ⁸ I will make the shadow cast by the sun go back the ten steps it has gone down on the stairway of Ahaz.'" So the sunlight went back the ten steps it had gone down. (Isaiah 38:7-8 - NIV)

5. Door Opened on its Own Accord

¹⁰ They passed the first and second guards and came to the iron gate leading to the city. It opened for them by itself, and they went through it. When they had walked the length of one street, suddenly the angel left him. (Acts 12:10 - NIV)

6. Philip Teleported

³⁹ When they came up out of the water, **the Spirit of the Lord suddenly took Philip away,** *and the eunuch did not see him again, but went on his way rejoicing. ⁴⁰ Philip, however, appeared at Azotus* *and traveled about, preaching the gospel in all the towns until he reached Caesarea.* (Acts 8:39-40 - NIV - Emphasis Added)

7. Jesus Walked on Water

²² Immediately Jesus made the disciples get into the boat and go on ahead of him to the other side, while he dismissed the crowd. ²³ After he had dismissed them, he went up on a mountainside by himself to pray. When evening came, he was there alone, ²⁴ and the boat was already a considerable distance from land, buffeted by the waves because the wind was against it. ²⁵ Shortly before dawn Jesus went out to them, walking on the lake. ²⁶ When the disciples saw him walking on the lake, they were terrified. "It's a ghost," they said, and cried out in fear. (Matthew 14:22-26 - NIV)

8. Snake Bite Ineffective

³ Paul gathered a pile of brushwood and, as he put it on the fire, a viper, driven out by the heat, fastened itself on his hand. ⁴ When the islanders saw the snake hanging from his hand, they said to each other, "This man must be a murderer; for though he escaped from the sea, the goddess Justice has not allowed him to live." ⁵ But Paul shook the snake off into the fire and suffered no ill effects. ⁶ The people expected him to swell up or suddenly fall dead, but after waiting a long time and seeing nothing unusual happen to him, they changed their minds and said he was a god. (Acts 28:3-6 - NIV)

9. Fire Burning but Not Consuming

[19] Then Nebuchadnezzar was furious with Shadrach, Meshach and Abednego, and his attitude toward them changed. He ordered the furnace heated seven times hotter than usual [20] and commanded some of the strongest soldiers in his army to tie up Shadrach, Meshach and Abednego and throw them into the blazing furnace. [21] So these men, wearing their robes, trousers, turbans and other clothes, were bound and thrown into the blazing furnace. [22] The king's command was so urgent and the furnace so hot that the flames of the fire killed the soldiers who took up Shadrach, Meshach and Abednego, [23] and these three men, firmly tied, fell into the blazing furnace. [24] Then King Nebuchadnezzar leaped to his feet in amazement and asked his advisers, "Weren't there three men that we tied up and threw into the fire?" They replied, "Certainly, Your Majesty." [25] He said, "Look! I see four men walking around in the fire, unbound and unharmed, and the fourth looks like a son of the gods." [26] Nebuchadnezzar then approached the opening of the blazing furnace and shouted, "Shadrach, Meshach and Abednego, servants of the Most High God, come out! Come here!" So Shadrach, Meshach and Abednego came out of the fire. (Daniel 3:19-26 - NIV)

10. Ten Plagues of Egypt

There were ten plagues that indicated to Egypt and its corrupt administration that there is a God who is alive, and that His Kingdom reigns above all else.

I. Water turned to blood (Exodus 7:17-18)
II. Abundant frogs from the river (Exodus 8:1-4)
III. Dust becomes lice (Exodus 8:16-17)
IV. Swarms of flies (Exodus 8:20-22)
V. Severe pestilence upon the animals (Exodus 9:1-4)
VI. Outbreak of tumors on man and animals (Exodus 9:8-9)
VII. Rain with severe thunder, hail and fire (Exodus 9:22-23)
VIII. Tree-eating locusts overcome the land (Exodus 10:4-5)
IX. Three-Day Black Out over the Land of Egypt (Exodus 10:21-22)
X. Death of the Egyptian's firstborn (Exodus 11:4-7)

11. Talking Donkey

²⁸ Then the Lord opened the donkey's mouth, and it said to Balaam, "What have I done to you to make you beat me these three times?" ²⁹ Balaam answered the donkey, "You have made a fool of me! If I had a sword in my hand, I would kill you right now." ³⁰ The donkey said to Balaam, "Am I not your own donkey, which you have always ridden, to this day? Have I been in the habit of doing this to you?" "No," he said. ³¹ Then the Lord opened Balaam's eyes, and he saw the angel of the Lord standing in the road with his sword drawn. So he bowed low and fell facedown. (Numbers 22:28-31 - NIV)

12. Joshua Stops the Sun

¹² On the day the Lord gave the Amorites over to Israel, Joshua said to the Lord in the presence of Israel: "Sun, stand still over Gibeon, and you, moon, over the Valley of Aijalon." ¹³ So the sun stood still, and the moon stopped, till the nation avenged itself on its enemies, as it is written in the Book of Jashar. The sun stopped in the middle of the sky and delayed going down about a full day. ¹⁴ There has never been a day like it before or since, a day when the Lord listened to a human being. Surely the Lord was fighting for Israel! (Joshua 10:12-14 - NIV)

13. Walls of Jericho Fall

¹⁶ The seventh time around, when the priests sounded the trumpet blast, Joshua commanded the army, "Shout! For the Lord has given you the city! ¹⁷ The city and all that is in it are to be devoted to the Lord.

Only Rahab the prostitute and all who are with her in her house shall be spared, because she hid the spies we sent. [18] *But keep away from the devoted things, so that you will not bring about your own destruction by taking any of them. Otherwise you will make the camp of Israel liable to destruction and bring trouble on it.* [19] *All the silver and gold and the articles of bronze and iron are sacred to the Lord and must go into his treasury."* [20] *When the trumpets sounded, the army shouted, and at the sound of the trumpet, when the men gave a loud shout, the wall collapsed; so everyone charged straight in, and they took the city.* [21] *They devoted the city to the Lord and destroyed with the sword every living thing in it – men and women, young and old, cattle, sheep and donkeys. (Joshua 6:16-21 - NIV)*

14. Noah Commands a Pair of All Animals to Enter the Ark

[17] *I am going to bring floodwaters on the earth to destroy all life under the heavens, every creature that has the breath of life in it. Everything on earth will perish.* [18] *But I will establish my covenant with you, and you will enter the ark – you and your sons and your wife and your sons' wives with you.* [19] *You are to bring into the ark two of all living creatures, male and female, to keep them alive with you.* [20] *Two of every kind of bird, of every kind of animal and of every kind of creature that moves along the ground*

will come to you to be kept alive. (Genesis 6:17-20 - NIV)

15. A Stick Becomes a Snake

³ The Lord said, "Throw it on the ground." Moses threw it on the ground and it became a snake, and he ran from it. ⁴ Then the Lord said to him, "Reach out your hand and take it by the tail." So Moses reached out and took hold of the snake and it turned back into a staff in his hand. (Exodus 4:3-4 - NIV)

16. Bears Created by Elisha's Words

²⁴ He turned around, looked at them and called down a curse on them in the name of the Lord. Then two bears came out of the woods and mauled forty-two of the boys. (2 Kings 2:24 - NIV)

These biblical accounts are true and trustworthy, and even history confirms that there are countless miracles that were done by other apostles in addition to what was accomplished by Paul.

But why don't we see these and other acts of God in this day and age? Why aren't miracles more prevalent today? Whatever our conclusions, we must know that all is not well with the Church as we know it. We must continue our search for answers.

Excuses We Give

Many have sought to explain why prayers are not answered; and we may not know the exact reason why this spiritual discipline has proven to be ineffective and unproductive for the most part. But we are allowed to speculate. The most basic and common reason is the **'Lack of Faith'**. When most people use this excuse, they mean that the intercessor did not truly *believe* that God would answer. Some would suggest that there was sin in the life of the person praying. Of course, if you search hard enough, you could find some form of sin in the life of *all* men. If this negative condition persists, then one may be deeply filled with guilt and shame and take the Church's 'anesthetic pill', go to sleep spiritually, and become paralyzed into non-activity.

Using the example of Daniel found in in Daniel 10:2-21, in which an angel fought his way through an intense 3-week battle in the heavenlies with the Prince of Persia to bring Daniel's answers to him, many postulate that demons are interfering with our prayers on a consistent basis. They contend that they are either blocking our prayers from reaching up to God or that they are stopping the answers from coming from Heaven. This truly elevates the power of demons to sublime levels. Even if that is the case for the individual believer, think of the billions of weekly prayers that are prayed and the number of demons it would take to do this. If this is so, then there would be no devil left to tamper with the other affairs of man.

It is evident that this level of spiritual resistance has been adopted by the enemy at times to delay answers to prayer

under the Old Covenant, but *after Calvary*, we are told that **Satan has been disarmed**:

> [15] And having **disarmed** the powers and authorities, he made a public spectacle of them, triumphing over them by the cross. (Colossians 2:15 - NIV - Emphasis Added)

I do not deny the existence of devils, but the writings of Paul do not carry a ***super-emphasis*** on Satan and his band of cohorts. He is a **defeated foe** and the weapons in which he trusted are **destroyed**! Paul also indicates that the believer has superior weapons.

> [3] *For though we live in the world, we do not wage war as the world does.* [4] *The weapons we fight with are not the weapons of the world. On the contrary, they have divine power to demolish strongholds.* (2 Corinthians 10:3-4 - NIV)

It is exciting to see what the Word of God says regarding the weapons that have been forged against us. This may be a lengthy quote, but it is worth looking at.

> [14] *You'll be built solid, grounded in righteousness, far from any trouble – nothing to fear! far from terror – it won't even come close!* [15] *If anyone attacks you, don't for a moment suppose that I sent them, And if any should attack, nothing will come of it.* [16] *I create the blacksmith who fires up his forge and makes a weapon designed to kill. I also create the destroyer –* [17] *but no weapon that can hurt you has ever been forged. Any accuser who takes you to court will be*

dismissed as a liar. This is what God's servants can expect. I'll see to it that everything works out for the best." God's Decree. (Isaiah 54:14-17 - MSG)

This passage establishes the following:

1. The believer is immovably grounded in the economy of the Kingdom.
2. The powers of the enemy do not even come close to being able to trouble them that serve God.
3. Anyone who attacks you are not sent by God, nor is their attack in the will of God.
4. God created the weapons and the warriors.
5. NO WEAPON that can overcome the Servant of God has EVER BEEN CREATED.

We give the devil more credit than is due. If there are billions of prayers each day and the enemy of our souls is able to provide such an impregnable barricade against them ascending to God's Throne, and then block the power of God from sending answers into the earth, then he packs more power than the entire Church worldwide. The text above shows us that **no weapon** that can overcome the child of God has ever been created.

In some cases, there are those who argue that prayers are not answered because the heavens are like brass. This means that God is in a non-responsive mode. A brassy Heaven is God judging the earth by not answering prayers. This may be true over a community of people, but over the entire Church as well? that is dubious. 2 Chronicles 7:13-16 addresses this issue.

> [13] "When I shut up the heavens so that there is no rain, or command locusts to devour the land or send a plague among my people, [14] if my people, who are called by my name, will humble themselves and pray and seek my face and turn from their wicked ways, then I will hear from heaven, and I will forgive their sin and will heal their land. [15] Now my eyes will be open and my ears attentive to the prayers offered in this place. [16] I have chosen and consecrated this temple so that my Name may be there forever. My eyes and my heart will always be there. (NIV)

God reveals in this passage of scripture that He is sometimes the cause of an economic downturn as a form of judgement for national sins. The term "When I shut up the heavens so that there is no rain..." gives us the idea of a brassy Heaven.

'Brass' in the Bible is a symbol of the judgement of God. Whenever the sky is as brass, the earth is always portrayed as iron. When the life of a people is under the judgement of God, the earth's economy is bad. When the sky is as brass, the prayers of a people are not as effective as they should be.

> [23] *The sky over your head will be bronze, the ground beneath you iron.* [24] *The Lord will turn the rain of your country into dust and powder; it will come down from the skies until you are destroyed.* (Deuteronomy 28:23-24 - NIV)

He further states that He is sometimes the one responsible for sending locusts to devour the land. The 'locusts' referred to here may be prototypical of demonic personalities.

It is easy for us to deduce here that **God** is the one causing the brassy heavens, as well as the locusts and plagues. Should we then accept that this is His perfect will for His people and stand idly by and do nothing? **God Himself**, in His lovingkindness and tender mercies, reveals the ***antidote*** to these condemnatory decrees of judgement by disclosing in the text that **a praying people can REVERSE the condition.**

> [14] **If MY people**, *who are called by* **MY** *name, will* **humble themselves** *and* **pray** *and* **seek my face** *and* **turn from their wicked ways, THEN I will hear from heaven,** *and* **I will forgive their sin** *and* **will heal their land**. (2 Chronicles 7:14 - NIV - Emphasis Added)

We can see clearly from this verse that 'prayer' coupled with 'righteousness' can reverse the spiritual climate over a people. For the purpose of emphasis, let us state this again. Even if God judges the land and stops answering prayer, the condition can be overruled and reversed by a praying people. Therefore, a brassy, closed up Heaven, should not be a persistent spiritual condition and a permanent excuse for unanswered prayer.

I must admit that my perspective of the problem may not necessarily represent that of mainstream Christianity. However, let me show you a few things. I think one of the problems is the 'size' of our prayers. Let me explain. It appears to me that prayer is a strategy designed to involve God in areas of life that reasonable human efforts cannot accomplish. We should not waste a lot of time and "faith capital" asking God to do the things **we** can do in a natural way. We see that in the ministry of Jesus: He prayed some very serious prayers. For example, let us dissect the prayer Jesus prayed in John chapter seventeen, and look at some of the items deemed important enough for Him to intercede regarding:

1. He determined the time for spiritual operations in the earth. Vs. 1 "the time is come..."

2. He established unity with a divine essence.

    [10] All I have is yours, and all you have is mine. And glory has come to me through them. [11] I will remain in the world no longer, but they are still in the world, and I am coming to you. Holy Father, protect them by the power of your name, the name you gave me, **so that they may be one as we are one.** (John 17:10-11 - NIV - Emphasis Added)

3. Equalization of mission with the Church and the Lord.

    [16] They are not of the world, even as I am not of it. [17] Sanctify them by the truth; your word is truth. [18] **As you sent me into the world, I have sent them into the world.** (John 17:16-18 - NIV - Emphasis Added)

The Church is not the offering for sin, neither is it the Savior of the world, but it possesses the same authority over the material universe and the works of the devil.

4. A prayer for everyone who would ever come into the Church—A prayer of global significance.

[20] "My prayer is not for them alone. I pray also for those who will believe in me through their message, [21] that all of them may be one, Father, just as you are in me and I am in you. (John 17:20-21 - NIV)

5. A prayer for a full revelation of GOD THE FATHER.

[25] "Righteous Father, though the world does not know you, I know you, and they know that you have sent me. [26] I have made you known to them, and will continue to make you known in order that the love you have for me may be in them and that I myself may be in them." (John 17:25-26 - NIV)

Big Prayers!!! Bold Prayers!!! Look at the men of old and how they challenged the supernatural. It was always in the context of major happenings. Look at the catalogue of men and women of the book of Hebrews. Through their prayers and faith, observe what these spiritual giants accomplished:

³² And what more shall I say? I do not have time to tell about Gideon, Barak, Samson and Jephthah, about David and Samuel and the prophets, ³³ who through faith conquered kingdoms, administered justice, and gained what was promised; who shut the mouths of lions, ³⁴ quenched the fury of the flames, and escaped the edge of the sword; whose weakness was turned to strength; and who became powerful in battle and routed foreign armies. ³⁵ Women received back their dead, raised to life again. There were others were tortured, refusing to be released, so that they might gain an even better resurrection. ³⁶ Some faced jeers and flogging, and even chains and imprisonment. ³⁷ They were put to death by stoning; they were sawed in two; they were killed by the sword. They went about in sheepskins and goatskins, destitute, persecuted and mistreated—³⁸ the world was not worthy of them. They wandered in deserts and mountains, living in caves and holes in the ground. (Hebrews 11:32-38 - NIV)

The Childish Sound, The Childish Tone

Very often, the typical prayer amounts to 'asking' with childish vocabulary and tonality. I have heard people in the Body of Christ pray all over the world with the tonality of a beggar. They ask with the sound of unworthiness and uncertainty. It is the sound of sin-consciousness and guilt. Furthermore, it is false humility. Some think that because they are praying to God, they should adopt a low octave and beggarly inflections in their voice. If this was an effective way to pray, then so many prayers would NOT go unanswered.

The Apostle Paul says in 1 Corinthians 13:10-12:

> *¹⁰ But when that which is perfect comes, then that which is imperfect shall pass away. ¹¹ When I was a child, I spoke as a child, I understood as a child, and I thought as a child. But when I became a man, I put away childish things. ¹² For now we see as through a glass, dimly, but then, face to face. Now I know in part, but then I shall know, even as I also am known.* (MEV)

He establishes that there is 'childish thinking', 'childish words' and 'childish understanding'. The context of his statement is against the perfect revelation of who we are before the Father. He projects into that which is perfect—but coming. He also points to a face-to-face encounter with God:

> *¹² For now [in this time of imperfection] we see in a mirror dimly [a blurred reflection, a riddle, an enigma], but then [when the time of perfection comes we will see reality] face to face. Now I know in part [just in fragments], but then I will know fully, just as I have been fully known [by God].* (1 Corinthians 13:12 (AMP)

Face-to-face with God is the level of full maturity, and not just seeing Him, but interacting with the Father from the place of perfection. It is this dimension we must seek for in our prayer lives.

In most families, parents are willing to give everything they can to their children. No good parent wants to hold back from the comfort and joy of their child. Yet they would abstain from doing so if what their children are asking for is outside the consideration of their level of maturity and responsibility. This would be evident in how they negotiate with you. Paul says there comes a time when we are to put away childish things.

Effective Praying sometimes means that we are to **CRY** out to the Lord. As much as crying depicts desperation and need, focus is placed several times in scripture on the concept of elevated volume and forcefulness. For example:

1. **Jabez 'called'**... (*quara* - Hebrew word) (1 Chronicles 4:10). This simply means that he raised the pitch and volume of his voice to God. He had asked God to stop pain and enlarge his territory. Later, God answered his prayer.

2. **The Men of Judah let out a war 'cry'**... (*ruwa* - Hebrew word) (2 Chronicles 13:15). This is an elevated noise; a sustained shout. It is characterized by a resolve to win and to destroy the enemy. It is a sound backed up by deadly intent. Look at the result, "it came to pass that God smote Jeroboam and all Israel." Judah prevailed.

3. **The Blind man 'implored'**... (*Boao* - Greek) (Luke 18:38-41). He yelled out "Jesus, thou

son of David, have mercy on me!" and he received his healing. His tonality was not childish and weak. It was a firm and loud expression of faith.

4. **Israel 'cried' unto the Lord in their bondage** (*za'ak* - Hebrew) (Exodus 2:23). This can be compared to the sound of a herald walking through the streets summoning the people to a public gathering. It is the sound of prayers that is calling upon God for an audience because of how grave the threat of danger is. This Prayer Dimension calls on God to actively join the discussion and act urgently. It is a call for a personal audience with the Most High.

Concerning the prayer life of the Lord Jesus, some of His prayers were configured by this dimension. Hebrews 5:7 says:

> *⁷ In the days of His flesh* **[Jesus]** *offered up definite,* **special petitions** *[for that which He not only wanted but needed] and* **supplications with strong crying and tears** *to Him Who was [always] able to save Him [out] from death,* **and He was heard** *because of His reverence toward God [His godly fear, His piety, in that He shrank from the horrors of separation from the bright presence of the Father].* (AMPC - Emphasis Added)

The other aspect to what I believe the answer to the question of: "What is the mystery of unanswered prayer?" is locked into the general content of this book. I will attempt to show that prayers which are configured by a persistent **begging** of God, seem to either be **left unanswered** or are marked by **great delay**. What we will find is, prayers that are strongly asking God for things, are those spent in surrender to God or configured by deep personal yieldedness. You will see the Lord in the Garden of Gethsemane sweating great drops of blood in prayer as He seeks to align His will to the Father. However, whenever He confronts the material world or demons, His prayers take on a new and different configuration of authority. The other chapters of this book will address this more thoroughly. Let's take this journey with an honest and open mind to learn a new and enhanced way to pray.

Prayer

Dearest Heavenly Father, I come to you in the name of the Lord Jesus. Thank you for your abundant provision of grace and for unhindered access to all that you have prepared for me. I honor you and love you with all my heart and pledge to serve you for the rest of time. Today I ask for the Spirit and the grace to aid me in my prayer life. Help me to build the discipline and skill to effectively approach you regularly. Grant me the spirit of supplication and prayer that I would live daily with an insatiable passion to pray.

Your Word declares that the effective, fervent prayer of a righteous man availeth much. Help me, then, to pray effectively and fervently. Your Word also declares that many ask and do not receive because they ask wrongly. Help me to ask correctly. May the words of my mouth

and the meditations of my heart be acceptable in Thy sight, oh Lord, My Redeemer. It is my desire to be the best intercessor that I can be. I want to rise to the pinnacle of prayer that I might reign and rule with you.

Help me to pray like Elijah; believe like Abraham; declare like David; prophecy like Daniel; weep like Jeremiah; and intercede like Jesus. Grant that my prayers be answered speedily and help me to effectively engage your supernatural power for signs and wonders. Let miracles be done in your name, and may hurting humanity be helped, and Christ be glorified. Use my prayers as a highway through which you can enter nations, towns and villages and perform your works with grace. Oh, that the unbelieving and the unchurched may be arrested through my prayers and turn to the Lord for salvation and be saved. These things I ask in Jesus' name, Amen.

NOTES

> "The concept of 'Altars' speaks of the practice and progression of 'Prayer' and defines significant movements into deeper levels of consecration to the Lord."

CHAPTER 2

Altars - Our Passage to His Presence

Understanding Altars

The concept of Altars is deeply rooted in biblical truth, as there are hundreds of references to it. Though they may be a physical object or location, they generally have to do with prayer, worship, sacrifice and consecration. We will expand on these concepts later. As we will see, Altars do not reflect the end of a journey, nor is it a place of finality or completion. We will see that they reflect stages of the journey in the Spirit, and not destinations. People do not stop at the Altar; they journey beyond them. This concept is of stupendous importance as we develop our understanding of prayer.

The concept of 'Altars' speaks of the practice and progression of 'Prayer' and defines significant movements into deeper levels of consecration to the Lord. Embedded in the revelation of Altars, are multiple layers of revelation regarding man's ascension to the realm of God. Hence, we need to build our understanding of them on this glorious adventure.

The online dictionary (*dictionary.com*) defines an 'Altar' as 'an elevated place or structure as a mound or platform at which religious rites are performed, or on which sacrifices are offered to gods or ancestors etc.' This, somewhat, fits into the biblical use of the word and it offers some interesting perspectives. The Altar is supposed to be an elevated place. The spiritual principle implied here is that of raised expectations and values. They are set up as if to acknowledge man's access to God. It becomes a place of high-level negotiations with the Father, and the receipt of infinite intelligence.

Another online dictionary (*webster.com*) adds to this definition. It states that 'an Altar is usually a raised structure or a place on which sacrifices are offered or incense burned in worship'. It is often used figuratively to describe a thing given greater or undue precedence or value, especially at the cost of something else. For example, "He sacrificed his family on the Altar of career advancement." In these definitions, we note that the Altar is, first of all, a place; then it is a dimension of relating to a deity, a god. Then we note later in this definition that *the Altar can be located in the heart*. This dimension is most important because it formulates how we pray; it shapes the intensity and the level of faith with which we pray. Therefore, the 'Altar Factor' that we are focused on is the dimension of prayer that we are most accustomed to. It is the standard one-way communication with God in which we ask God for things and believe that His answers are contingent on our works—our ability to win His favor.

Biblically speaking, the word 'Altar' first appears when Noah built the Altar and sacrificed animals on it after the Flood. The word for 'Altar' here is the Hebrew word '*mizbeach*' [pronounced *miz-bay-ekh*]. It literally means 'to kill'. In this sense, Altars are places of death. Beyond the 'Altar Dimension' is the flow of 'divine life'. Dr. Vine, in *"Vine's Expository of Old Testament Words,"* explains that Altars were to be made of a table of stone or ground. This signifies that an Altar had to be from substance that was strictly of divine formation. This meant that the 'Altar Dimension' is where our function had to be according to the specific requirements of God, and that God would not respond to us if we are not praying, worshipping or sacrificing according to those specifications.

Dr. Vine further opines that whenever the human had to shape the Altar, God did not want them to use instruments of war. This is what He said:

> ²⁵ *If you make an altar of stones for me, do not build it with dressed stones, for you will defile it if you use a tool on it.* ²⁶ *And do not go up to my altar on steps, or your private parts may be exposed.'* (Exodus 20:25-26 - NIV)

Herein are two important factors on forming a powerful foundation for effective prayer. Firstly, effective prayer is made from a heart that is brutally honest with God. One is not to dress the stones used for the Altar. Use the stones as you find them. Altar prayers are rough and crude in expression. We are to kill all pretense and hypocrisy. Secondly, develop and maintain sexual purity to ascend the heights of prayer. They were not allowed to climb Altars and show the shame of adultery, fornication, homosexuality, bestiality, necrophilia, prostitution and the such like. The implication here is the shame before God for the battery of sexual sins. It is clear in this little passage that one cannot have power with God when living in sexual sin. You cannot climb the Altars of prayer if you are living in persistent sexual sins.

Horns of the Altar

Until we come to the Tabernacle of Moses, God was usually not the one initiating Altars. Based on the language used in scripture, we notice that prior to this, it was generally "this one or that one" who took it upon themselves to build an Altar to the Lord. Whatever truths we can derive from that, we cannot justly say that this is of God's original design. However, when God instructed Moses to build the two Altars in the Mosaic System of Worship, He hid special truths there for us to capture. Though we will not consider them all in this discourse, we will consider this one: The Altars that God instructed Moses to make had four 'horns' on them. 'Horns' are symbols of 'Power'. This indicates that there is awesome power to the Altar Dimension of prayer. In my understanding, here are the four powers of the Altar:

1. **The Power of Death [crucifying the old man].** Within the economy of Moses, Altars are bloody places. In the times of worship, thousands of animals would be slaughtered. This was analogous of the final Lamb—Jesus the Christ—that was to be slain for our redemption. However, as we capture the Prayer Factor of the Altar, we must accept that it is also a place where our 'old self' died with Christ. This may be somewhat passive in our thinking, but in the Spirit and in the realm of divine perspectives, the death of the old self is **critical** to our ability to function in the divine.

Paul argues that we are crucified with Christ:

[20] I have been crucified with Christ and I no longer live, but Christ lives in me. The life I now live in the body, I live by faith in the Son of God, who loved me and gave himself for me. (Galatians 2:20 - NIV)

When we bow our hearts in prayer and faith in the Lord Jesus, figuratively speaking, we are holding on to the horns of the Altar. That is, we activate and deploy the power of God to mortify the old self and its way of life.

And again, the great Apostle admonishes us, as it were, to keep that old self upon the Altar of death.

[5] Put to death, therefore, whatever belongs to your earthly nature: sexual immorality, impurity, lust,

evil desires and greed, which is idolatry. ⁶ Because of these, the wrath of God is coming. ⁷ You used to walk in these ways, in the life you once lived. ⁸ But now you must also rid yourselves of all such things as these: anger, rage, malice, slander, and filthy language from your lips. ⁹ Do not lie to each other, since you have taken off your old self with its practices ¹⁰ and have put on the new self, which is being renewed in knowledge in the image of its Creator. (Colossians 3:5-10 - NIV)

Note how he refers to the 'old nature' as the 'earthly nature'. This means that it is low and weak in the things of God. It means that it lacks the capacity to reliably operate in the things of the Spirit of God and so must be put to death. The Amplified version of the Bible makes it a bit more understandable:

⁵ So kill (deaden, deprive of power) the evil desire lurking in your members [those animal impulses and all that is earthly in you that is employed in sin]: sexual vice, impurity, sensual appetites, unholy desires, and all greed and covetousness, for that is idolatry (the deifying of self and other created things instead of God). (Colossians 3:5 - AMPC)

The essence of this revelation is that when we bow our hearts in prayer with regards to our relationship with God, we place our lives on the Altar of sacrifice and terminate the power of inbred sin. Then, at the same time, we take on newness of life in Christ. Having identified with Him in His death, burial and resurrection, we rise to walk in newness of life. Through this Altar Dimension of prayer, we are releasing the power of His resurrection. At the Altar, we unleash the character of Christ in our hearts, giving us the propensities to do the will of God and to enjoy righteousness.

God commanded Israel to never let the fire on the Altar go out.

⁸ The Lord said to Moses: ⁹ "Give Aaron and his sons this command: 'These are the regulations for the burnt offering: The burnt offering is to remain on the altar hearth throughout the night, till morning, and **the fire must be kept burning on the altar**. (Leviticus 6:8-9 - NIV - Emphasis Added)

God was advocating that the death of the old self was to be an eternal experience, and that the believer was to walk eternally in newness of life. Continual fires upon the Altar of God was to signal to us: that which was slain on the Altar was never to be resurrected. As we lay our lives on this Altar of death to the old self, we are to continually establish that the old self, with all its lusts, is kept in subjection.

2. **The Power of Surrender [bending the will].** At the Altar of sacrifice, we surrender our will to the Lord. Through this violent dimension

of prayer, we are **bending** our will towards His. We are forcing our will to conform to His will. Please note that this is a Prayer Factor. As we will observe, prayer is not just asking God for fame and fortune. It is also petitioning the grace of God to enable us to please Him.

Let us take a look at the Lord Jesus in Gethsemane. In a real sense, what He experienced was an Altar Prayer Dimension, and perhaps the most graphic in the entire Bible.

⁴⁰ On reaching the place, he said to them, "Pray that you will not fall into temptation." ⁴¹ He withdrew about a stone's throw beyond them, knelt down and prayed, ⁴² "Father, if you are willing, take this cup from me; **yet not my will, but yours be done."** (Luke 22:40-42 - NIV - Emphasis Added)

Here our Lord points to two wills. The first was the will of the Father in redeeming the human race. There were two facets to this: the first is God's love for the human race; and second and most importantly, is His 'method' of bringing salvation to the earth. His method was to save the world through the suffering and ultimate death of the Lord Jesus.

But it was not forced upon the Lord. It was dependent on Christ surrendering **His** will to that of the Father. Christ was aware of the awesome pain in His body and spirit as He was being prepared to become the ultimate sin offering. He entered into such deep agony that His sweat became as drops of blood as He travailed—not for things, we must emphasize—but so that He could joyfully surrender to the Father's will. This indeed is one of the horns of the Altar. Before coming into the world, He had already agreed to do God's will.

⁷ Then said I, **Lo, I come** *(in the volume of the book it is written of me,)* **to do thy will, O God***. ⁸ Above when he said, Sacrifice and offering and burnt offerings and offering for sin thou wouldest not, neither hadst pleasure therein; which are offered by the law; ⁹ Then said he,* **Lo, I come to do thy will, O God.** *He taketh away the first, that he may establish the second.* (Hebrews 10:7-9 (KJV) Emphasis Added)

This prayer of surrender is one that every child of God should master. It forces upon the intercessor the sense of self-abandonment and sacrifice of one's agenda and preferences for that which is God's. There is in every one of us, the violent conflict—no matter how great we are or how mature we are in God—the vulnerability to sin and the possibility to become enslaved to it. At this point we must move to the Altar without arrogance and pride, but in deep submission and brokenness. We must pray and wait till the victory is won and sin's power is broken in us.

We often spend prolonged time fighting demons at the proverbial Altar. But that is not what the Altar is for. The horns of the Altar unleash power to break our stubborn will and provoke yieldedness to God. There is an old song we used to sing. Its words speak pointedly to this matter:

My Stubborn will at last hath yielded;
I would be thine and thine alone,
And this the prayer my lips are bringing
Lord, let in me thy will be done.

Sweet will of God, still fold me closer,
Till I am wholly lost in thee;
Sweet will of God, still fold me closer,
Till I am wholly lost in thee.

Shut in with thee, O Lord, forever.
My wayward feet no more to roam;
What pow'r from thee my soul can sever?
The center of God's will my home.

3. **The Power of Consecration.** As there are four horns on the Altar, there are four dimensions of power that Altar Prayers produce. The 'Dimension of Consecration' is one of them.

When we pray prayers of consecration and dedication, we function at the Altar. We may call this the 'prayer of committal'.

Essentially, we are committing ourselves to a sacred purpose. In the Garden of Gethsemane, our Lord was not only bending His will to obey and comply with that of the Father, but He was dedicating Himself to His purpose on the earth, namely, dying on the Cross. His prayer was a prayer of consecration and dedication. We must do this periodically as the routines of life wear upon our hearts and souls. We should pause at the Altar to pray and ask God to strengthen our hearts and hands for the task. These prayers provoke the power of God in us, working and producing a righteous resolve to suffer and to endure ridicule, shame, need and opposition for the Glory of God.

Such was the resolve of the Apostle Paul. Even when the prophet Agabus warned him of impending danger to his ministry in Jerusalem, he refused to take the path of least resistance but strove manfully forward, despising the shame. He echoed Acts 20:24:

[24] *But none of these things move me, neither count I my life dear unto myself, so that I might finish my course with joy, and the ministry, which I have received of the Lord Jesus, to testify the gospel of the grace of God.* (KJV)

Though the New Covenant does not allow us to build physical Altars, it requires the *inner* elevated place of sacrifice and dedication. I am afraid that we have not known this place—it is unfamiliar to us. This generation of fun-loving, game-loving, entertainment-loving Christians amongst whom we live do not understand this. We have come to glorify the profiteering of goods and services within the environs of the Kingdom without valuing true spiritual formations.

We find musicians that would not settle in a local church without pay. Preachers who would only visit certain places because of the honorarium. We have members hopping from church to church without endurance, or allowance of time to be 'made' by God. We have spiritual babies who could pray and prophesy, fragmenting local churches while disseminating pettiness and rebellion. Their hearts are shallow and void of true development. There is no wonder that we have beautiful edifices for churches, silky smooth administration, but **no power**! Church services have become a nest for gays, lesbians, transvestites and transsexuals. Mind you, I am not denying the right of these persons to be in the house of God. I am just saying that there is no *real power* that convicts of sin and of righteousness and of judgment to come. One of the reasons there is no power is because there is no Altar.

Figuratively speaking, and in sharp contrast to God's instructions, our Altars have **many steps** that allow the "underwear" of the ministers to be revealed. Entertainers entertain the fickle and the profane. This Altar Dimension is the place of seriousness and earth-shattering gravity of soul. It is the place of godly fear. The question is: **Have you been** to the Altar? A better question is: **Are you going** to the Altar? Even better yet: **When** will you go there? Let me add another question: **How long** will you spend there?

Allow me to linger here for a moment, because the light-heartedness of our people stays the hand of God and of His blessing. Ezekiel deals with this matter of the consecrated life, as he journeys through the house of God in a vision to get to the Altar. God directed him to a hole in the wall:

⁷ Then he brought me to the entrance to the court. I looked, and I saw a hole in the wall. ⁸ He said to me, "Son of man, now dig into the wall." So I dug into the wall and saw a doorway there. (Ezekiel 8:7-8 - NIV)

This means that there are detestable things happening in people's lives that are masked and hidden by the walls we put up to hide our sins. But God found a way for the prophet to see. There are some ministries that look great on the outside, but if only we can find a hole to look through, we would find **detestable** things.

God showed the prophet a *false* cloud of Glory in the lives of the people.

¹¹ᵇ Each had a censer in his hand, and a fragrant cloud of incense was rising. (Ezekiel 8:11b - NIV)

In their iniquitous state, they made an attempt to manufacture the 'Glory cloud'. But where there is no true consecration, there can be no power. When we are disingenuous with consecration, we produce spurious power.

4. **The Power of Daily Provision.** The word used for 'Altar' also means to 'slaughter for food'. It indicates that there is a place in which we petition God so as to have food for each day. At the Altar, we ask God for our daily bread and for His provision for each day's sustenance. The priest typically would eat of the thing sacrificed, and so this may be what was meant by "slaughter for food."

However, I choose to believe that the deeper and more accurate understanding would be that through the power of the Altar Dimension of prayer, one's individual economy is favorably affected. Because it related to the individual's sacrifice, it would bear specifically on one's daily provision of food. Altar-type prayer provides food for brief periods and not necessarily in great abundance. It does not impact on the macro levels of a nation's economy. It is not designed to raise the Gross Domestic Product. The Altar Dimension of prayer is not designed to move a person into stratospheric levels of prosperity. Nevertheless, it is necessary for a person to start here.

Scripture admonishes us to cast our cares upon the Lord.

[6] Humble yourselves, therefore, under God's mighty hand, that he may lift you up in due time. 7 Cast all your anxiety on him because he cares for you. (1 Peter 5:6-7 - NIV)

It further advises us to trust the Lord for each day's supply.

[6] Do not be anxious about anything, but in everything, by prayer and petition, with thanksgiving, present your requests to God. [7] And the peace of God, which transcends all understanding, will guard your hearts and your minds in Christ Jesus. (Philippians 4:6-7 - NIV)

This is what the Altar Dimension does for us. It provides us with grace for each day's supply. Here is where the majority of people live, and this is not offensive to God. But it is functioning **way below** our privileges and covenantal rights.

Holding on to the Horns of the Altar

"Clinging to the horns of the Altar" or "holding on to the horns of the Altar" have been clichés in the Church world for many years now. It means to persist in prayer until the answer comes. Often, when in trouble, a good Pentecostal mother may tell you, "Hold on brother" or "hold on my child," "hold on to the horns of the Altar." This concept of 'persistence in prayer' is a strong spiritual principle. However, we must note that several times when "holding on to the horns of the Altar" was mentioned in scripture, it was being done in fear.

In the following case, Joab was running in fear and clung to the horns of the Altar, fearful for his life.

> ^{28} *Then tidings came to Joab: for Joab had turned after Adonijah, though he turned not after Absalom. And Joab fled unto the tabernacle of the Lord, and caught hold on the horns of the altar.* (1 Kings 2:28 - KJV)

Fearful that Saul would take his life, Adonijah fled to the house of God and clung to the horns of the Altar.

> ^{49} *At this, all Adonijah's guests rose in alarm and dispersed. ^{50} But Adonijah, in fear of Solomon, went and took hold of the horns of the altar. ^{51} Then Solomon*

was told, "Adonijah is afraid of King Solomon and is clinging to the horns of the altar. He says, 'Let King Solomon swear to me today that he will not put his servant to death with the sword.'" (1 Kings 1:49-51 - NIV)

Although we see value here—in that when our hearts are overwhelmed with fear, prayer has the incredible power to change our responses to circumstances and also eliminate the threat—we must also see that this dimension is not that which unleashes uncommon miracles and history-altering events. Those who clung to the Altar were typically praying in fear and not faith. Such is the state of the Church.

Beyond the Altar

I believe that there is a dimension of prayer which before now has not gained the prominence that it should. I am not postulating that I am the origin of the concept. There are those who before now called it the 'Prayer of Command', or 'Governmental Prayer', or the 'Prayer of Decree'. All of these descriptions have accuracy, but I want to place it deeply in the sea of biblical truth and inspire the Body of Christ to a new and improved way to pray.

The chief mention of the Altar Factor is in the Tabernacle of Moses. In the Mosaic System of worship there were two Altars: The Brazen Altar and the Altar of Incense. Both of them speak to dimensions of prayer. We are not going to give an elaborate exposition on the subject of the Brazen

Altar, nor dig too deeply into the values of the Golden Altar of Incense. What is of importance to our conversation is that both Altars are located in the path of the priest to the Holiest of Holies where the Throne of God is.

As mentioned before, prior to the Tabernacle of Moses, Altars were usually built by man's initiative. For the most part, they were built by people whose lives were in transition. This principle is important as it is central to our concern. God provided an organized revelation of the Altar in the Mosaic System of worship. This, we must admit, was of God's design and, therefore, must be the basis of truth. The priest followed the protocol to access the presence of God.

First, he was to slaughter the animals at the Brazen Altar of sacrifice. Remember that the word 'altar' speaks of 'death'. It also means 'to slaughter for food'. Then he washes at the Brazen Laver. We will look at this truth a bit later. For now, though, note that he is not cleansing from sin at the Brazen Laver. He is washing himself from the blood that is now on him from the many animals that he had slaughtered. To be cleansed from the blood is an amazing truth. However, he then enters the Holy Place.

According to the book of Hebrews, there are three pieces of furnishings here. The first is the Golden Lampstand. Remember that at this point the priest is in a dark place, so light is now necessary. More than that, though, the light shines in the room but also on the second piece of furniture—the table of shewbread—and the priest is allowed to eat this. Many have spiritualized this to impractical levels. However, the light of God speaks of illumination or education. Knowledge is referred to here. God provides knowledge and it shows us how to get bread. The third piece of furnishing is the Golden Altar of Incense. The incense is used to clear the air of the stench of blood as one is entering the glorious presence of God. It shows us the deep and powerful force of prayer, for it is this dimension that ushers man into the abiding presence of God. God told the priest that, "At this place, I will meet you."

There is a significant difference between praying at the Brazen Altar and praying at the Golden Altar of Incense. At the Brazen Altar, the intercessor is acutely conscious of his deep need for salvation, surrender, and consecration. At the Brazen Altar (slaughter for food) he is also conscious of his need to have God take care of his most basic necessities such as food, clothing and shelter.

This second Altar is not brassy—it is Golden. At this place the man is no longer focused on the damaging effects of sin. Hence, the aroma is different, and the appearance is different. He is now praying and worshipping God, not for what he wants, but for what God has done. He is at the place of finished realities. Here he is not thinking as a vagrant nor a pauper. He thinks like royalty, and he prays accordingly. May we all joyfully celebrate the wonderful deliverance and relationship we have with our Heavenly Father; and may our conversations with Him be elevated to sublime heights.

Prayer

Great and Glorious Father, I bow my heart in prayer to you this day. My heart is forever grateful for your merciful plan of redemption. Through the finished work of Christ, my sins have been atoned for. Through this plan I have been bought with a price, not silver nor gold, but the Precious Blood of the Lord Jesus. I am thankful that on the Cross of Calvary, He died in my place. He took the punishment for my sins that I may be free. He took my sickness and give me His health. He took my poverty and gave me His riches. I praise you, Lord, for being my substitute, my sacrifice and my scapegoat. Through the death of my Savior, the just demands of God have been satisfied and I have entered into a new and lasting covenant with God.

Now I proclaim before Heaven and earth that Jesus is my Savior and Lord. I declare the I am His, and He is mine. I have the life of God in me; I am born again, and my name is written in the Lamb's Book of Life. All my sins are forgiven and the new life I now live, I live by faith in the Son of God who loves me and gave Himself for me.

Now I am freed from the tyrannical rule of Satan. Death has no power over my life and every curse is personally broken. Through the power of inbred righteousness, I live above sin and walk in the righteousness of God. Sin does not have dominion over me. I walk each day in the love and wisdom of God.

I have strength for all things in Christ who empowers me. I am ready for anything and equal to anything through Him who infuses inner strength into me; I am self-sufficient in Christ's sufficiency.

Grant me the courage and the faith to move my life and prayers beyond the Altar to the Throne without losing the power of a life lived in total submission to your will. I pledge to follow you wherever you may lead me, and to grow in grace and in the knowledge of Christ. I pray these things in faith, believing, in Jesus' name. Amen.

NOTES

> "THERE IS A PLACE BEYOND THE 'ALTAR DIMENSION' OF PRAYER. **THE THRONE.** THAT IS THE ULTIMATE PLACE TO WHICH WE MUST GO."

CHAPTER 3

Beyond the Altars

Earlier, we made reference to the fact that the people who were building Altars were pilgrims, or men and women in transition. Some of them were actually in physical transition as well. Others were in a place of spiritual transition. By understanding this, we are saying that the Altar Dimension is not the most advanced way to pray. We are establishing that there is a dimension beyond this, and we are all journeying to that place in a personal developmental way. Also, the Global Church is maturing to this place of advanced prayer and mature participation with God. Let's examine some cases of men who built Altars.

Noah Built an Altar to Transition Mankind from The Place of Judgment to A New World Order or A New Dispensation

[20] *Then Noah built an altar to the Lord and, taking some of all the clean animals and clean birds, he*

sacrificed burnt offerings on it. ²¹ The Lord smelled the pleasing aroma and said in his heart: "Never again will I curse the ground because of humans, even though every inclination of the human heart is evil from childhood. And never again will I destroy all living creatures, as I have done. (Genesis 8:20-21 - NIV)

Abraham Built an Altar to The Lord to Consecrate Himself and His Children to The Purposes of God, and to Bring About Spiritual Shifts in The Earth

God had activated a devoted man to function strictly by promise and faith.

⁶ Abram traveled through the land as far as the site of the great tree of Moreh at Shechem. At that time the Canaanites were in the land. ⁷ The Lord appeared to Abram and said, "To your offspring I will give this land." So he built an altar there to the Lord, who had appeared to him. ⁸ From there he went on toward the hills east of Bethel and pitched his tent, with Bethel on the west and Ai on the east. There he built an altar to the Lord and called on the name of the Lord. ⁹ Then Abram set out and continued toward the Negev. (Genesis 12:6-9 - NIV)

Isaac Built an Altar Signaling the Changing of The Guards

God now continues His redemptive plan through a new person: Isaac.

²³ From there he went up to Beersheba. ²⁴ That night the Lord appeared to him and said, "I am the God of your father Abraham. Do not be afraid, for I am with you; I will bless you and will increase the number of your descendants for the sake of my servant Abraham." ²⁵ Isaac built an altar there and called on the name of the Lord. There he pitched his tent, and there his servants dug a well. (Genesis 26:23-25 - NIV)

Jacob Built an Altar on His Way Back Home to Celebrate the Victories of God Over His Past Failures

He called the name of the place 'El Elohe Israel' or 'the Mighty One of Israel' (Jacob's name was changed to Israel).

¹⁸ After Jacob came from Paddan Aram, he arrived safely at the city of Shechem in Canaan and camped within sight of the city. ¹⁹ For a hundred pieces of silver, he bought from the sons of Hamor, the father of Shechem, the plot of ground where he pitched his tent. ²⁰ There he set up an altar and called it El Elohe Israel. (Genesis 33:18-20 - NIV)

Moses Built an Altar to The Lord to Celebrate the Victory Over the Obstacle of Amalek.

¹⁴ Then the Lord said to Moses, "Write this on a scroll as something to be remembered and make sure that Joshua hears it, because I will completely blot out the memory of Amalek from under heaven." ¹⁵ Moses built an altar and called it The Lord is my Banner. ¹⁶ He said, "Because hands were lifted up against the throne of the Lord, the Lord will be at war against the Amalekites from generation to generation." (Exodus 17:14-16 - NIV)

Balaam Built Seven Altars to Obtain Blessing for The Israelites Who Had Stopped, En Route, To Their Promised Land

At this point a heathen King named Balak wanted the prophet to curse the people of God. Balaam's Altar prevented the prophetic curse.

> *¹ Balaam said, "Build me seven altars here, and prepare seven bulls and seven rams for me." ² Balak did as Balaam said, and the two of them offered a bull and a ram on each altar. ³ Then Balaam said to Balak, "Stay here beside your offering while I go aside. Perhaps the Lord will come to meet with me. Whatever he reveals to me I will tell you." Then he went off to a barren height. ⁴ God met with him, and Balaam said, "I have prepared seven altars, and on each altar I have offered a bull and a ram." ⁵ The Lord put a message in Balaam's mouth and said, "Go back to Balak and give him this word." ⁶ So he went back to him and found him standing beside his offering, with all the Moabite officials. ⁷ Then Balaam spoke his message: "Balak brought me from Aram, the king of Moab from the eastern mountains. 'Come,' he said, 'curse Jacob for me; come, denounce Israel.' ⁸ How can I curse those whom God has not cursed? How can I denounce those whom the Lord has not denounced?* (Numbers 23:1-8 - NIV)

Joshua Built an Altar to Establish That They Had Crossed Over into The Land of Promise

> ² When you have crossed the Jordan into the land the Lord your God is giving you, set up some large stones and coat them with plaster. ³ Write on them all the words of this law when you have crossed over to enter the land the Lord your God is giving you, a land flowing with milk and honey, just as the Lord, the God of your fathers, promised you. ⁴ And when you have crossed the Jordan, set up these stones on Mount Ebal, as I command you today, and coat them with plaster. ⁵ Build there an altar to the Lord your God, an altar of stones. Do not use any iron tool on them. ⁶ Build the altar of the Lord your God with fieldstones and offer burnt offerings on it to the Lord your God. ⁷ Sacrifice fellowship offerings there, eating them and rejoicing in the presence of the Lord your God. ⁸ And you shall write very clearly all the words of this law on these stones you have set up. (Deuteronomy 27:2-8 - NIV)

David Built an Altar to The Lord to Deal with The Condition of His Heart in Provoking A Plague in The Land

He had sacrificed the peace of Israel on the Altar of his own pride.

> ¹⁸ On that day Gad went to David and said to him, "Go up and build an altar to the Lord on the threshing floor of Araunah the Jebusite." ¹⁹ So David went up, as the Lord had commanded through Gad. ²⁰ When

Araunah looked and saw the king and his men coming toward him, he went out and bowed down before the king with his face to the ground. ²¹ Araunah said, "Why has my lord the king come to his servant?" "To buy your threshing floor," David answered, "so I can build an altar to the Lord, that the plague on the people may be stopped." ²² Araunah said to David, "Let my lord the king take whatever he wishes and offer it up. Here are oxen for the burnt offering, and here are threshing sledges and ox yokes for the wood. ²³ Your Majesty, Araunah gives all this to the king." Araunah also said to him, "May the Lord your God accept you." ²⁴ But the king replied to Araunah, "No, I insist on paying you for it. I will not sacrifice to the Lord my God burnt offerings that cost me nothing." So David bought the threshing floor and the oxen and paid fifty shekels of silver for them. ²⁵ David built an altar to the Lord there and sacrificed burnt offerings and fellowship offerings. Then the Lord answered his prayer in behalf of the land, and the plague on Israel was stopped. (2 Samuel 24:18-25 - NIV)

Elijah Built an Altar to The Lord to Eliminate A False Prophetic Order from The Land

He sought to bring Israel to a new place of worship and godly fear of God.

> *²⁷ At noon Elijah began to taunt them. "Shout louder!" he said. "Surely he is a god! Perhaps he is deep in thought, or busy, or traveling. Maybe he is sleeping and must be awakened." ²⁸ So they shouted louder*

and slashed themselves with swords and spears, as was their custom, until their blood flowed. ²⁹ Midday passed, and they continued their frantic prophesying until the time for the evening sacrifice. But there was no response, no one answered, no one paid attention. ³⁰ Then Elijah said to all the people, "Come here to me." They came to him, and he repaired the altar of the Lord, which had been torn down. ³¹ Elijah took twelve stones, one for each of the tribes descended from Jacob, to whom the word of the Lord had come, saying, "Your name shall be Israel." ³² With the stones he built an altar in the name of the Lord, and he dug a trench around it large enough to hold two seahs of seed. ³³ He arranged the wood, cut the bull into pieces and laid it on the wood. Then he said to them, "Fill four large jars with water and pour it on the offering and on the wood." ³⁴ "Do it again," he said, and they did it again. "Do it a third time," he ordered, and they did it the third time. ³⁵ The water ran down around the altar and even filled the trench. ³⁶ At the time of sacrifice, the prophet Elijah stepped forward and prayed: "Lord, God of Abraham, Isaac and Israel, let it be known today that you are God in Israel and that I am your servant and have done all these things at your command. ³⁷ Answer me, O Lord, answer me, so these people will know that you, Lord, are God, and that you are turning their hearts back again." ³⁸ Then the fire of the Lord fell and burned up the sacrifice, the wood, the stones and the soil, and also licked up the water in the trench. ³⁹ When

all the people saw this, they fell prostrate and cried, "The Lord–he is God! The Lord–he is God!" ⁴⁰ *Then Elijah commanded them, "Seize the prophets of Baal. Don't let anyone get away!" They seized them, and Elijah had them brought down to the Kishon Valley and slaughtered there.* (1 Kings 18:27-40 - NIV)

Careful observation of the passages above show that these Altars were made as the people of God were geographically moving or were dealing with some major spiritual transition. As the Old Testament is a system of 'shadows' and 'types', we can deduce that their system of prayer reflected the Kingdom in its fetal or embryonic position. Their system of prayer was not divinely instructed as we see in the teachings of the New Covenant.

¹³ When you were dead in your sins and in the uncircumcision of your flesh, God made you alive with Christ. He forgave us all our sins *¹⁴ having canceled the charge of our legal indebtedness, which stood against us and condemned us; he has taken it away, nailing it to the cross.* *¹⁵* **And having disarmed the powers and authorities, he made a public spectacle of them, triumphing over them by the cross.** *¹⁶ Therefore do not let anyone judge you by what you eat or drink, or with regard to a religious festival, a New Moon celebration or a Sabbath day. ¹⁷ These are* **a shadow** *of the things that were to come; the reality, however, is found in Christ.* (Colossians 2:13-17 - NIV - Emphasis Added)

This passage establishes that the defeat of Satan is an authentic spiritual reality and that we are forgiven of all of our sins, legitimizing our righteousness and privileges. Our life is now a genuine outflow of the life of God and cannot be regulated or judged by Old Testament rites and ceremonies.

Those Altars built by travelers, by pilgrims, and searching souls represent a prayer life that was not trained and equipped by the revelations of the New Testament. For this reason, the Lord spoke of the greatness of John the Baptist in this way:

> *[11] Truly I tell you, among those born of women there has not risen anyone greater than John the Baptist; yet whoever is least in the kingdom of heaven is greater than he.* (Matthew 11:11 - NIV)

There was never a prophet nor citizen under the Old Covenant who walked in the greatness of John, yet the least person in the Kingdom of God in this current dimension is greater than John.

It is hard to decode what the Lord meant when He said that. It would appear that He was referencing the position and privilege factors. We all know that those in the New Testament access things that are better, and this too we will examine. But consider this:

> *[12] From the days of John the Baptist until now, the kingdom of heaven has been advancing forcefully and forceful people are seizing it. [13] In fact, all the prophets and the law prophesied until John. [14] If you are willing to receive it, he is the Elijah who was to come. [15] Whoever has ears to hear, let him hear.* (Matthew 11:12-15 - EHV)

Jesus may have been referencing the attitude of John the Baptist in relation to the Kingdom. He was a forceful man and produced a level of forcefulness in prayer. When he prayed, he prayed with an attitude of forcefulness that produced the mighty move of God, the advent and ministry of Christ the Messiah.

Furthermore, and to establish my point, you will observe that he taught others to pray in the same way.

> *¹ One day Jesus was praying in a certain place. When he finished, one of his disciples said to him, "Lord, teach us to pray,* **just as John taught his disciples***." ² He said to them, "When you pray, say: "'Father, hallowed be your name, your kingdom come. ³ Give us each day our daily bread. ⁴ Forgive us our sins, for we also forgive everyone who sins against us. And lead us not into temptation.'"* (Luke 11:1-4 - NIV - Emphasis Added)

It appears that John used to teach his disciples to pray differently from the way Jews would normally pray. His prayers evidently were *forceful.* This may have been the divine tool that spiritually prepared the way for the Messiah to do His work.

I would seriously contend that the Altar Prayers of those who walked with God prior to that era, were not well constructed. They were prayers that were not based upon solid revelation of the plans and purposes of God. They were prayers that were founded on an imperfect spiritual and redemptive system. As history progressed and the Kingdom Community learnt more of God—and having the combined witness of all the men and women of God that went before us—we can pray more effectively.

No Doors Behind the Holiest of Holies

The tabernacle in the wilderness is a graphical display of the established protocol for approaching the presence of God. God had told Moses to build it according to the pattern revealed from Heaven by the Lord Himself.

> ⁹ *According to all that I shew thee, after the pattern of the tabernacle, and the pattern of all the instruments thereof, even so shall ye make it.* (Exodus 25:9 - KJV)

God had revealed to Moses in an emblematic way how man could approach God successfully. The system of the tabernacle that he built had incredible spiritual principles, instructing man how to access the supernatural realm; the Shekinah Glory of God that is around the Throne.

Note that there was a gate through which one could enter the Outer Court. As the priest enters the Outer Court, he encounters the Brazen Altar. This represents the most basic practices of Prayer. As we learnt, it is the level where our sins—the most incredible barrier to God—are dealt with. This is not just a reference to the death of Jesus on the Cross, as this cannot redeem man by itself. It represents **our prayerful application of the provisions of Calvary**. Here we pray the prayers of consecration and dedication.

Then there is an access doorway through which the priest must go to get into the Holy Place.

> *¹ Now the first covenant had regulations for worship and also an earthly sanctuary. ² A tabernacle was set up. In its first room were the lampstand and the table with its consecrated bread; this was called the Holy Place. ³ Behind the second curtain was a room called the Most Holy Place, ⁴ which had the golden altar of incense and the gold-covered ark of the covenant. This ark contained the gold jar of manna, Aaron's staff that had budded, and the stone tablets of the covenant. ⁵ Above the ark were the cherubim of the Glory, overshadowing the atonement cover. But we cannot discuss these things in detail now. ⁶ When everything had been arranged like this, the priests entered regularly into the outer room to carry on their ministry. ⁷ But only the high priest entered the inner room, and that only once a year, and never without blood, which he offered for himself and for the sins the people had committed in ignorance. ⁸ The Holy Spirit was showing by this that the way into the Most Holy Place had not yet been disclosed as long as the first tabernacle was still standing. ⁹ This is an illustration for the present time, indicating that the gifts and sacrifices being offered were not able to clear the conscience of the worshiper. ¹⁰ They are only a matter of food and drink and various ceremonial washings—external regulations applying until the time of the new order.* (Hebrews 9:1-10 - NIV)

After praying the prayers of dedication, and cleansing of the spirit and soul from the power of inbred sin, the priest must now progress into the literal presence of God to learn to function at a greater level. In this place he is to learn to minister to God with a new vocabulary, a new attitude, a new faith and new purpose. The lampstand would shine its light upon the table where there was bread. Bread, then and now, symbolized the level of man's material provision. The light of God in the Holy Place was designed to produce bread or wealth in a man's life.

Beyond this place, according to the passage in Hebrews that we read, was the Holiest of Holies. This is what was called the Most Holy Place because it represents the place of God's Throne. In this place was the Ark of the Covenant and the Golden Altar of Incense. We must note that to get there, the priest had to go beyond the veil. This place in the Tabernacle of Moses represents a dimension of prayer and relationship with God that is **the ultimate place to which we must go.** Here, prayer is most effective and most glorious. In the Throne Room is a Golden Altar of Incense. This speaks of worship and prayer. **At the Throne, everything changes for the saint. He has to learn to pray as a King.** At this place, he is not petitioning God as if he were a beggar. God would not respond. *Here* he is to function as a master of devils and a master over the material universe. It is from this dimension he executes the judgments written by God over the nations. From this place, he can change times and seasons. Prayer is no longer begging God. **This dimension is the issuance of decrees and declarations.** This is what we must understand. There is no way out of this place except you reverse. There is no door beyond this place. This is it. This is the ultimate level of Prayer. It is the place that God wants us all to come.

In the Throne Room, we are *like* God and we *represent* God to the world. It is the disposition of our original design. Man was created to live daily in the presence of God. His was the privilege to live in Eden, the place of God's abiding presence. It is the place of a glorious relationship and fellowship with God. Adam was made in the image and the likeness of God. This meant that he was created to be like God, and to represent God. As it took God thousands of years to make the way to the Most Holy Place available to man, we must know how serious this is to Him. From the language of the New Testament, we know that the New Covenant is superior in every way to that of the Old.

It is Based Upon a Superior Sacrifice

[1] The law is only a shadow of the good things that are coming – not the realities themselves. For this reason it can never, by the same sacrifices repeated endlessly year after year, make perfect those who draw near to worship. [2] Otherwise, would they not have stopped being offered? For the worshipers would have been cleansed once for all, and would no longer have felt guilty for their sins. [3] But those sacrifices are an annual reminder of sins. [4] It is impossible for the blood of bulls and goats to take away sins. [5]

Therefore, when Christ came into the world, he said: "Sacrifice and offering you did not desire, but a body you prepared for me; ⁶ with burnt offerings and sin offerings you were not pleased. ⁷ Then I said, 'Here I am—it is written about me in the scroll—I have come to do your will, my God.'" ⁸ First he said, "Sacrifices and offerings, burnt offerings and sin offerings you did not desire, nor were you pleased with them"— though they were offered in accordance with the law. ⁹ Then he said, "Here I am, I have come to do your will." He sets aside the first to establish the second. ¹⁰ And by that will, we have been made holy through the sacrifice of the body of Jesus Christ once for all. (Hebrews 10:1-10 - NIV)

A Superior Sanctuary

¹¹ But when Christ came as high priest of the good things that are now already here, he went through the greater and more perfect tabernacle that is not made with human hands, that is to say, is not a part of this creation. (Hebrews 9:11- NIV)

It is Based Upon a Superior Priesthood

¹ This Melchizedek was king of Salem and priest of God Most High. He met Abraham returning from the defeat of the kings and blessed him, ² and Abraham gave him a tenth of everything. First, the name Melchizedek means "king of righteousness";

then also, "king of Salem" means "king of peace." ³Without father or mother, without genealogy, without beginning of days or end of life, resembling the Son of God he remains a priest forever. (Hebrews 7:1-3 - NIV)

¹¹ If perfection could have been attained through the Levitical priesthood—and indeed the law given to the people established that priesthood—why was there still need for another priest to come, one in the order of Melchizedek, not in the order of Aaron? ¹² For when the priesthood is changed, the law must be changed also. ¹³ He of whom these things are said belonged to a different tribe, and no one from that tribe has ever served at the altar. ¹⁴ For it is clear that our Lord descended from Judah, and in regard to that tribe Moses said nothing about priests. ¹⁵ And what we have said is even more clear if another priest like Melchizedek appears, ¹⁶ one who has become a priest not on the basis of a regulation as to his ancestry but on the basis of the power of an indestructible life. ¹⁷ For it is declared: "You are a priest forever, in the order of Melchizedek." (Hebrews 7:11-17 - NIV)

It is Based Upon Superior Promises

⁶ But in fact the ministry Jesus has received is as superior to theirs as the covenant of which he is mediator is superior to the old one, since the new covenant is established on better promises. (Hebrews 8:6 - NIV)

It Provided Superior Faith and Assurance

¹⁶ Men indeed swear by a greater [than themselves], and with them in all disputes the oath taken for confirmation is final [ending strife]. **¹⁷ Accordingly God also, in His desire to show more convincingly and beyond doubt to those who were to inherit the promise the unchangeableness of His purpose and plan, intervened (mediated) with an oath.** *¹⁸ This was so that, by two unchangeable things [His promise and His oath]* **in which it is impossible for God ever to prove false or deceive us,** *we who have fled [to Him] for refuge might have mighty indwelling strength and strong encouragement to grasp and hold fast the hope appointed for us and set before [us]. ¹⁹ [Now] we have this [hope] as a sure and steadfast anchor of the soul [it cannot slip and it cannot break down under whoever steps out upon it – a hope] that reaches farther and enters into [the very certainty of the Presence] within the veil, [Leviticus 16:2.] ²⁰ Where Jesus has entered in for us [in advance], a Forerunner having become a High Priest forever after the order (with the rank) of Melchizedek. [Psalm 110:4.]* (Hebrews 6:16-20 - AMPC - Emphasis Added)

Dear reader, we note that in the books of the New Testament we see that **no one** is building Altars. Through the terms and provisions of this new relationship with God, we pray with a new boldness and new faith. Altars are bloody places of death. At the Throne, there is the beautiful aroma of freedom and life. We do not pray as paupers or beggars or strangers. Here we issue decrees and declarations as kings. Around the Throne, we are not bound by sin or live with guilt and shame. Here is the place where we pray without a sin-consciousness. Here our God-Consciousness is superior over our sin-consciousness.

At the Altar we are journeying. At the Throne, we arrive and pray as such. Altars reflect prayers that are prayed from a place of immaturity. **In the Throne Room, we pray as mature sons.** Altar prayers reflect the Church in its embryonic fetal posturing. At Altars, we pray without full awareness of the plans and purposes of God. Beyond the Altar, we pray with the thoughts of God. At the Altar, we are fearful, but **we come boldly to the Throne of Grace** to negotiate with the King of Kings. Here in the Throne Room we get to see and know the schematics of redemption and God's plans for the ages. Here we pray from the place of *finished realities*.

Prayer

Glorious Father, I come to you in praise and thanksgiving. Your name is holy and you are perfect in all your ways. I worship you because you do all things well.

My Father, your domain, your Kingdom, is a borderless domain because of the number of its inhabitants, its wealth and its indescribable power. Your Kingdom is borderless because of its fire and glory. No one can withstand nor restrict your purposes and plans. Your Kingdom is an everlasting kingdom, and a vast domain.

Because of its vastness, I understand and agree that all I know is not all I can know. All the things that man has done, are not all there is to do. All the frontiers that can be visited have not yet been visited. All the miracles that can be done, have not as yet been accomplished. All the songs and plays that can be written, have not been written. Yours is a vast domain.

Therefore, Holy Father, I set my heart on pilgrimage. I set my heart to journey to the next level of performance, impact and productivity. In you I live and move. So, I pledge to relocate my life in you to new heights of prayer and intercession. I will listen to your Word and follow where you lead. I will allow your Spirit to reveal your plans and purposes to me and hearken to your voice.

Master of my soul, I deny the forces of religion, tradition and unbelief to restrict and confine me to the practices and ways of the past. I will not pray the same prayers in the same ways. I choose today not to use the same prayer points and attitudes of former

years. I choose to shift from begging for the things that you have already provided. I acknowledge that I am your Child and I am not, nor will I ever be, a pauper. I will not pray as a peasant, but rule as a king upon the earth.

I thank you for the journeys of my ancestors of the Faith and for the examples that they have set for me in their relationship with you. But I hear the clarion call for the Bride of Christ to climb the dizzy heights of intercession in the heavenlies and arise in faith to minister before you from that place. So, come, oh Lord, to my aid and usher me to that place. Teach me to pray in the Throne Room. Equip me to issue commands, decrees and declarations upon the earth, insisting that the earth comply with your plans and purposes. In the name of the Lord Jesus Christ I pray. Amen.

> "HOLDING ON TO THE HORNS OF THE ALTAR MEANS THAT WE MAINTAIN THE BASIC PRINCIPLES AND COMPONENTS OF PRAYER."

CHAPTER 4

Holding On To the Horns of the Altar

We have established that the Altar Dimension of prayer is the most basic level of intimacy with God. I will argue that *it is an absolutely necessary dimension and must not be destroyed.* Often, in current moves of God, we find a skewed understanding of what it means to grow or to advance in God. Most think and act as if moving on in Him is to abandon past moves or established principles.

To move on to perfection can be compared to constructing a building. In the construction of a new edifice, one wants to get to the roof and do all the finishing touches. However, you never leave the foundation undone. Foundational doctrines such as Sanctification, Justification and Glorification are not obsolete, and should continue to be taught in current operations of God. Even the word 'doctrine' seems to have taken on a spiritually backward connotation in some faith-based environments. The word 'doctrine' simply refers to the order of God or the way that God wants things done.

As it relates to the Altar Dimension of prayer, we will note that it speaks to the foundational approaches to God and also to basic guiding principles of prayer. The Bible teaches us that one can be taught how to pray.

> *¹ One day Jesus was praying in a certain place. When he finished, one of his disciples said to him,* "**Lord, teach us to pray**, *just as John taught his disciples.*"
> (Luke 11:1 - NIV - Emphasis Added)

In this passage of scripture, we see that the disciples *saw* their Lord in prayer, and they **heard** Him pray. We can glean from this verse that effective intercession can be observed in the use of the body, vocabulary and emotions. Considering that the disciples grew up as Jews and must have known about prayer, it is safe to conclude that they saw something that was **new** and **instructive**. Additionally, they referenced the prayer culture of John the Baptist and that of his followers, so they must have had some knowledge of prayer. Then they asked the Lord to **teach them to pray** as John taught his disciples. They were not asking the Lord to teach them to pray the same way that John's disciples prayed. They were asking the Lord to do for them what John did for his disciples. The disciples wanted to learn to pray in the 'Jesus' way.

The fact that the Lord did not upbraid them by saying that teaching others to pray is preposterous, tells us that it

is possible to teach others to pray after a particular order. John had an order and he mentored his followers to pray on that wise. Furthermore, the Lord proceeded to give them a pattern of prayer that can be used as a teaching tool for effective intercession. This prayer is the 'Jesus Dimension' and not John's. Therefore, we must conclude that not only can one be **taught** how to pray, but that there are certain **elementary and advanced principles** of effective prayer.

When we speak of "holding on to the horns of the Altar," we are talking about strict adherence to the fundamental principles of intercession and a commitment to build on them. So, what we have known about prayer is not all there is to know. To shut out any new or advanced principles of intercession is the fossilize ourselves and to be lost in antiquity. As we used to say in classical Pentecostalism: "there are deeper depths, and higher heights in God," to which we must go. We used to sing:

1. Deeper, deeper in the love of Jesus
Daily let me go;
Higher, higher in the school of wisdom,
More of grace to know.

REFRAIN:
Oh, deeper yet, I pray,
And higher every day,
And wiser, blessed Lord,
In Thy precious, holy Word.

2. *Deeper, deeper, blessed Holy Spirit,*
   Take me deeper still,
   Till my life is wholly lost in Jesus,
   And His perfect will.

3. *Deeper, deeper! though it cost hard trials,*
   Deeper let me go!
   Rooted in the holy love of Jesus,
   Let me fruitful grow.

4. *Deeper, higher, every day in Jesus,*
   Till all conflict past,
   Finds me conqu'ror, and in His own image
   Perfected at last.

I believe that this day is indeed upon us. We are to move to a new place in God where greater results are had. Let's boldly carry on and apprehend this new place courageously.

For us then, holding on to the horns of the Altar means that we maintain the basic principles and components of prayer. We are not to become so advanced that we ignore and scoff at those who uses these principles. To establish the fundamentals of prayer, we will point to issues of Promises, Postures and Principles.

Promises, Promises

The Word of God presents glorious and precious promises guaranteeing us answers to our prayers. These promises

contain the strongest expressions of affirmation possible in any language. You will notice promissory phrases in scripture such as: "it *shall* be given," "*shall* find," and so on. God seeks to provide not only a strong motivation for us to pray, but also a strong confidence that **He will answer**.

You shall Receive, Discover and Access

7 "Ask and it will be given to you; seek and you will find; knock and the door will be opened to you. 8 For everyone who asks receives; the one who seeks finds; and to the one who knocks, the door will be opened. 9 "Which of you, if your son asks for bread, will give him a stone? 10 Or if he asks for a fish, will give him a snake? 11 If you, then, though you are evil, know how to give good gifts to your children, **how much more will your Father in heaven give good gifts to those who ask him!** (Matthew 7:7-11 - NIV - Emphasis Added)

This promise establishes that our prayers will generate answers to questions and petitions. It also establishes discovery and revelation. 'Seeking' in the passage is the dimension of prayer that is intended to bring originality to goods and services. Prayer will invent things. It will create entrepreneurs and intrapreneurs. If you seek, you will find. Also, prayer is intended to provide access. In this instance, prayers will get you beyond doors of nations, laws, barriers and institutions. It will provide skillful ways to circumvent protocols designed to make access difficult.

Answers Promised to an Unlimited Scope of Requests

God promised to answer all the things we ask for and whatever we ask in the name of Jesus.

> ^{22} *And all things, whatsoever ye shall ask in prayer, believing, ye shall receive."* (Matthew 21:22 - KJV)

> ^{13} *And whatever you ask in My name, that I will do, that the Father may be glorified in the Son.* ^{14} *If you ask anything in My name, I will do it.* (John 14:13-14 - NKJV)

> ^{23} *In that day you will not question Me about anything. Truly, truly, I say to you, if you ask the Father for anything in My name, He will give it to you.* ^{24} *Until now you have asked for nothing in My name; ask and you will receive, so that your joy may be made full.* (John 16:23-24 - NASB)

He Not Only Promised to Give You Your Needs, but also Your Wishes (Wants)

> ^{7} *If you abide in Me, and My words abide in you, ask whatever you wish, and it will be done for you.* (John 15:7 - NASB)

He Promised to Answer Prayers That Produce Creativity for New Goods and Services

> ^{16} *You did not choose Me but I chose you, and appointed you that you would go and bear fruit, and that your fruit would remain, so that whatever you*

ask of the Father in My name He may give to you. (John 15:16 - NASB)

He Promised to Answer, To Respond to Our Questions

14 "Because he has loved Me, therefore I will deliver him; I will set him securely on high, because he has known My name. 15 "He will call upon Me, and I will answer him; I will be with him in trouble; I will rescue him and honor him. 16 "With a long life I will satisfy him And let him see My salvation." (Psalm 91:14-16 - NASB)

He Promised to Answer When We Call, When We Bid Him to Come

14 "Offer to God a sacrifice of thanksgiving And pay your vows to the Most High; 15 Call upon Me in the day of trouble; I shall rescue you, and you will honor Me." (Psalm 50:14-15 - NASB)

God Will Even Answer the Prayer of the HEART Sometimes Not Made Audible

17 O LORD, You have heard the desire of the humble; You will strengthen their heart, You will incline Your ear. (Psalm 10:17 - NASB)

God Will Hear Prayers Made from The Place of Our Pain (Painful Prayers)

22 You shall not afflict any widow or orphan. 23 If you afflict him at all, and if he does cry out to Me, I will surely hear his cry; (Exodus 22:22-23 - NASB)

God Is Searching the Earth Looking for Prayers to Answer, Because Some Prayers Are Not Effective

[19] For He looked down from His holy height; From heaven the LORD gazed upon the earth, [20] To hear the groaning of the prisoner, To set free those who were doomed to death, (Psalm 102:19-20 - NASB)

God Responds to Prayers That Are Prayed in Sincere Desperation

[17] The afflicted and needy are seeking water, but there is none, And their tongue is parched with thirst; I, the LORD, will answer them Myself, As the God of Israel I will not forsake them. (Isaiah 41:17 - NASB)

God Will Answer the Prayers That Reverse Divine Judgement

This means that, no matter how sinful the person or how severe the judgement, prayers can even alter divine negative decrees and verdicts.

[14] and if My people who are called by My name humble themselves and pray and seek My face and turn from their wicked ways, then I will hear from heaven, will forgive their sin and will heal their land. (2 Chronicles 7:14 - NASB)

God Will Answer Prayers That Alter the Demographics of The Land

[37] 'Thus says the Lord GOD, "This also I will let the house of Israel ask Me to do for them: I will

increase their men like a flock. (Ezekiel 36:37 - NASB)

God Answers Prayers of Restoration

⁶ "I will strengthen the house of Judah, And I will save the house of Joseph, And I will bring them back, Because I have had compassion on them; And they will be as though I had not rejected them, For I am the LORD their God and I will answer them. (Zechariah 10:6 - NASB)

God Will Answer Prayers That are Prayed to Perfect Character

⁸ "It will come about in all the land," Declares the LORD, "That two parts in it will be cut off and perish; But the third will be left in it. ⁹ "And I will bring the third part through the fire, Refine them as silver is refined, And test them as gold is tested. They will call on My name, And I will answer them; I will say, 'They are My people,' And they will say, 'The LORD is my God.'" (Zechariah 13:8-9 - NASB)

God Answers Prayers by Those That Please Him

²²and whatever we ask we receive from Him, because we keep His commandments and do the things that are pleasing in His sight. (1 John 3:22 - NASB)

God Answers Prayers Prayed Over Our Faith Projects

²⁴ "Therefore I say to you, all things for which you pray and ask, believe that you have received them, and they will be granted you. (Mark 11:24 - NASB)

¹⁴ This is the confidence which we have before Him, that, if we ask anything according to His will, He hears us. (1 John 5:14 - NASB)

God Promised to Answer Prayers Made in Agreement

¹⁹ "Again I say to you, that if two of you agree on earth about anything that they may ask, it shall be done for them by My Father who is in heaven. (Matthew 18:19 - NASB)

Guaranteed Answers to Prayer

We have been given concrete assurances from the Word of God itself, solidified by the character of God and a moving cloud of witnesses, that God **will** answer our prayers. Because faith is so very vital when it comes to answered prayers, and because we cannot activate the power of God without faith, the Bible creates the spiritual context for faith. We do not have to doubt for a second that the things we ask for in prayer would not be given. We should not halt between two opinions regarding this matter. We should not yield to human ideas and opinions on these spiritual matters. Indeed, we are to let God be true and every man a liar. The first thing we are to know is the integrity of the Word.

1. The Integrity of His Word

a. God's Word Cannot Return to Him Void

[10] As the rain and the snow come down from heaven, and do not return to it without watering the earth and making it bud and flourish, so that it yields seed for the sower and bread for the eater, [11] so is my word that goes out from my mouth: It will not return to me empty, but will accomplish what I desire and achieve the purpose for which I sent it. (Isaiah 55:10-11 - NIV)

This passage uses a powerful natural process to establish our assurance in God's Promises. Rain and snow have been falling out of the heavens since the days of Adam. No one has ever seen them hesitate nor retreat back into the clouds. No one has ever seen them change their mind. Once they are released from the heavens, one can be guaranteed that they would land on the ground. It does not matter how light or heavy they may be. It does not matter the temperature or their distance from the ground. Eventually they will hit the earth.

The snow nor the rain do not consider the earthly conditions or the earth's readiness for them. So it is with the Word of God—it carries the same certainty of accomplishing what it was sent out to do. The conditions of the earth or its readiness is of no consequence to the Lord. They come from the mind and the heart of God and so He already assessed the circumstances and configured the Word to fulfill **His** purposes. Consequently, the Word will not and *cannot* return to Him void.

b. **God Watches Over His Word to Perform It**

^{11} The word of the Lord came to me saying, "What do you see, Jeremiah?" And I said, "I see a rod of an almond tree." ^{12} Then the Lord said to me, "You have seen well, for I am watching over My word to perform it." (Jeremiah 1:11-12 - NASB)

God told the prophet to look at the almond tree, and, as if disjointed in thought, He told Jeremiah that He, God, is watching over His word to see that it is fulfilled. This is quite interesting. In those days, it was customary for dry twigs from the almond tree to be used as a stick which a blind man used to tap his way through a path.

I believe the Lord was using this analogy to say that even if He lost His sight, He would ensure—like a blind man—that He taps His way through time and situations to make sure that His good promises are fulfilled in the life of all prospective recipients. Delivery on His promises are guaranteed.

2. He Would Not Break His Covenant

²⁸ I will maintain my love to him forever, and my covenant with him will never fail. ²⁹ I will establish his line forever, his throne as long as the heavens endure. ³⁰ "If his sons forsake my law and do not follow my statutes, ³¹ if they violate my decrees and fail to keep my commands, ³² I will punish their sin with the rod, their iniquity with flogging; ³³ but I will not take my love from him, nor will I ever betray my faithfulness. **³⁴ I will not violate my covenant** *or alter what my lips have uttered. ³⁵ Once for all, I have sworn by my holiness—and I will not lie to David— ³⁶ that his line will continue forever and his throne endure before me like the sun; ³⁷ it will be established forever like the moon, the faithful witness in the sky."* (Psalm 89:28-37 - NIV - Emphasis Added)

God's commitment to us is based upon His eternal love. As simple as this may sound, we must know the incredible significance that this has. His desire to bless us is not regulated by human weakness or character, but rather, upon the basis of His love for us all. Then God explicitly says, "My covenant I will NEVER break." All the terms of the covenants that He has ever made are ***guaranteed*** to come to pass. God promised David that someone from his household would always be king in Judah. However, there is no guarantee that they would all please God like David did. God says something very special here. He said that even if David's children lived in sin, they could not stop the precious promises of God from coming to pass.

Should it become necessary, God agrees to deal with their sin problem by punishing them, whilst also preserving the integrity of His word. That means the punishment of God would not wipe them out, leaving David without a legacy. He promised to judge them without killing them. The punishment, then, would be restorative and redemptive; and not excessively painful and final. He has to keep them alive, so He could fulfill His word. Amazing and satisfying. So, in our lives God may punish us for wrongdoing, but it is never final. He would preserve us until He has done all that He has promised to us. He sustains us for His promise sake.

Additionally, God's promises are sworn oaths. He adds swearing to the promise. Whereas either a promise or an oath can stand alone, in order to provide us with an absolute guarantee, God adds an 'oath' to the 'promise'. In the above passage the Lord states that He *swore* by His Holiness. This means that to break His word makes Him a sinner. When He promised, it is as if He placed Himself at the risk of becoming as a fallen man.

He also stated that He would never betray His faithfulness. The reason that had to be said can be seen in the context of the conversation. He pointed to the possibility of unfaithfulness in the lineage of David. God was saying that even when the house of David—or we can apply it to us—even when **we** are not faithful to Him, He abides faithful to us.

3. Heaven and Earth Shall Pass Away

^{17} Think not that I am come to destroy the law, or the prophets: I am not come to destroy, but to fulfil. ^{18} For

verily I say unto you, Till heaven and earth pass, one jot or one tittle shall in no wise pass from the law, till all be fulfilled. (Matthew 5:17-18 - KJV)

This verse is quite interesting. God is affirming us of the surety of His word by declaring that whatever He says would come to pass before Heaven and earth go out of existence. But from the study of the scriptures, this is definitely **not** going to happen. Our eschatology states that God will create a new Heaven and a new earth–in the sense of renovation. He will purify the material universe as we know it. But they will last forever. He could not possibly mean that all He promised would be fulfilled and that the world would cease to exist.

God is showing us here that even if the world were to be destroyed prematurely, He would reassemble the entire world to make His good word come to pass. If by any stroke of our imagination some rogue leader in one of our nuclear-powered nations starts a thermonuclear war and completely obliterates the entire planet; if every life ends and the world is blown to smithereens and scattered throughout the expanse of the Universe; then if God remembers that He promised you or me something that did not materialize, He would go to the extent of reassembling the entire world, resurrecting every human necessary, recreating every animal, and replacing every required element in the world to make His good word come to pass. What an incredible assurance; what incredible power behind His word. We have no reason to doubt His word; we have no reason to hesitate in the face of the problems of life. God most certainly would make His promises come to pass.

4. The Integrity of His Character

a. He Is Not Like Man to Lie

¹⁹ God is not human, that he should lie, not a human being, that he should change his mind. Does he speak and then not act? Does he promise and not fulfill? ²⁰ I have received a command to bless; he has blessed, and I cannot change it. (Numbers 23:19-20 - NIV)

Here we have insight into the person of God. It establishes that God does not have a defiled character, and that He keeps His word. He does not deceive us nor trick us into action. He means what He says, and He says what He means. We can take Him at His word every time He speaks.

Not only does God not lie—He simply would **not** change His mind about His promises. We can rest in this assurance that God is not going to look on our failures and then decide He is going to alter His promises. Since He is **all-knowing**, we can be well-assured that when He made the promises, He was also knowledgeable of prevailing obstacles ahead of time and took them into consideration when He spoke.

As a result, there should be no misfortune to be found amongst the people of God. The implication is that His promises are good and not promises to do us harm. They provide assurance of the abundant supply of God.

b. There Is No Shadow of Turning in Him

12 Blessed is the man that endureth temptation: for when he is tried, he shall receive the crown of life, which the Lord hath promised to them that love him. 13 Let no man say when he is tempted, I am tempted of God: for God cannot be tempted with evil, neither tempteth he any man: 14 But every man is tempted, when he is drawn away of his own lust, and enticed. 15 Then when lust hath conceived, it bringeth forth sin: and sin, when it is finished, bringeth forth death. 16 Do not err, my beloved brethren. 17 Every good gift and every perfect gift is from above, and cometh down from the Father of lights, **with whom is no variableness, neither shadow of turning.** (James 1:12-17 - KJV - Emphasis Added)

The first expressions in this passage encourages us to persist for the things we desire even when we are in bad circumstances or faced with our own mistakes. The attempt of Apostle James is to compare and contrast the character of man with the character of God. Essentially, he is saying that we change with the shifting fortunes of life. We fail, we change, we are tossed around, and we are sometimes unable to meet the standards set by God—we fall short of His glory. Notwithstanding that, God has not changed in His person or His Character. He is not like man subject to the shifting fortunes of life.

Shadows change with the slightest movement of light. Light speaks of new insights and ideas. God, though, does not change when new perspectives come, or research and statistics arrive at new conclusions. He is all knowing. All of the things He has promised or spoken are done so against the backdrop of His omniscience. When He spoke, He knew our condition: past, present, and future. IF He changed because we changed, then He deceived us—and we know He would not do that. In God there is no variation of His character. Once we have come to know Him, then that is who He is: unchangeable in all His ways.

c. **He Is the Same Yesterday, Today, and Forever**

⁶ So we say with confidence, "The Lord is my helper; I will not be afraid. What can mere mortals do to me?" ⁷ Remember your leaders, who spoke the word of God to you. Consider the outcome of their way of life and imitate their faith. ⁸ **Jesus Christ is the same yesterday and today and forever**. (Hebrews 13:6-8 - NIV - Emphasis Added)

The assurance of the unfailing nature of the Lord's character is intended to move us to a place of confident speech. Our decrees, prayers and declarations are to be done with absolute confidence. That is, we are to speak with the assurance that God's Word will come to pass just as HE said. This assurance is to deliver us from fear. We should not be afraid that our faith would bring us to shame. This is because of the unfailing nature of the character of God. We are well assured that the same God who worked with Adam, Moses, Elijah, Joshua, Abraham, Isaac and Jacob, is the same God who worked with the Great Prophets and Apostles of old. And it is He who also works with us today. We can rest assured that He will be to us what He was to them, and more, because we have a covenant based upon **better** Promises.

This is a legal argument based upon presidency. Within the construct of jurisprudence, we can argue a case with God. We can say that if He was a miracle-working and a wonder-working God to Moses, then He ought to be to us too. If He answered the prayers of Elijah then, He can answer us as well today.

d. He Does Not Change

¹ "I will send my messenger, who will prepare the way before me. Then suddenly the Lord you are seeking will come to his temple; the messenger of the covenant, whom you desire, will come," says the Lord Almighty. ² But who can endure the day of his coming? Who can stand when he appears? For he will be like a refiner's fire or a launderer's soap. ³ He will sit as a refiner and purifier of silver; he will purify the Levites and

refine them like gold and silver. Then the Lord will have men who will bring offerings in righteousness, *⁴ and the offerings of Judah and Jerusalem will be acceptable to the Lord, as in days gone by, as in former years. ⁵ "So I will come to put you on trial. I will be quick to testify against sorcerers, adulterers and perjurers, against those who defraud laborers of their wages, who oppress the widows and the fatherless, and deprive the foreigners among you of justice, but do not fear me," says the Lord Almighty. ⁶ "I the Lord do not change. So you, the descendants of Jacob, are not destroyed. ⁷ Ever since the time of your ancestors you have turned away from my decrees and have not kept them. Return to me, and I will return to you," says the Lord Almighty...* (Malachi 3:1-7 - NIV)

e. **God Cannot Lie**

¹³ When God made his promise to Abraham, since there was no one greater for him to swear by, he swore by himself, ¹⁴ saying, "I will surely bless you and give you many descendants." ¹⁵ And so after waiting patiently, **Abraham received what was promised**. *¹⁶ People swear by someone greater than themselves, and the oath confirms what is said and puts an end to all argument. ¹⁷ Because God wanted to make the unchanging nature of his purpose very clear to the heirs of what was promised, he confirmed it with an oath. ¹⁸ God did this so that, by two unchangeable things in which* **it is impossible for God to lie**, *we who have fled to take hold of* *the hope offered to us may be greatly encouraged. ¹⁹ We have this hope as an anchor for the soul, firm and secure. It enters the inner sanctuary behind the curtain, ²⁰ where our forerunner, Jesus, has entered on our behalf. He has become a high priest forever, in the order of Melchizedek.* (Hebrews 6:13-20 - NIV - Emphasis Added)

These things are too wonderful for us. The Bible states unambiguously that it is impossible for God to lie and He cannot change. This truth provides an absolute basis for faith. We can trust in the integrity of God when we make declarations or make petitions. Here we notice, too, that our provisions and blessings are sure. The use of this word implies that there is no possibility, there is no external circumstance nor internal condition that can hinder God from doing what He said.

We also note that God says His purpose is unchanging. What He plans to accomplish in your life by abundantly supplying you and by replenishing you, will be achieved. His purposes in your life will be done. He planned before time to bless you and to lavish you with His favor.

⁷ In him we have redemption through his blood, the forgiveness of sins, in accordance with the riches of God's grace ⁸ that he lavished on us. With all wisdom and understanding, ⁹ he made known to us *the mystery of his will according to his good pleasure, which he purposed in Christ, ^{10} to be put into effect when the times reach their fulfillment—to bring unity to all things in heaven and on earth under Christ.* (Ephesians 1:7-10 - NIV)

We are to take into account that throughout time, with all its shifting fortunes, God knew beforehand what failures we would undergo. He knew all of our mistakes, yet He made promises and spoke purpose over our lives. He cannot change His mind after He promised, because when He did so, He did so with the knowledge of our weaknesses.

^{28}*And we know that all things work together for good to them that love God, to them who are the called according to his purpose.* (Romans 8:28 - KJV)

The text in Hebrews 6:13-20 affirms a number of factors. Firstly, **the promise**. The promise is the initial utterance that God made to Abraham to bless him. That one declaration was enough, and God needed not to speak another word to him to reaffirm anything. Yet God **swore** on the promise as well. Note, we have **an oath** and **a promise**. The oath, according to the text, is intended to end all doubt. The writer speaks in human terms. The reference can be compared to a man making a contract with another. The contract is the 'promise'; the 'oath' is the guarantee or the collateral. It ends any and all strife. It bears comparison with when a man swears on the Bible to tell the truth: the *truth* told is one thing, but the *oath* makes the man impeachable in the conventional judicial systems. It ends all doubts, fears, and hesitations.

This affirmation of blessing puts God in an impeachable position, so to speak. He is obligated to honor His word to you or He commits an impeachable offense. This means that the heirs of promise would become his God, and He would be our servant.

The other basis of faith is not explicitly stated, but it is implied, and our deduction does not violate the text nor violate New Covenant theology. He points to the Lord Jesus going beyond the veil. The reference is to the finished work of Christ at Calvary. The reference is to the power of the blood and of the sacrifice of Christ for our sins. The ultimate reason for altering His promise to us is our sins. Remember that no situation external to God's ideological position can be shifted in God to stop the blessing. The only blockage can come from the sins of man. Therefore, His work on the Cross is the ultimate guarantee of the blessing.

The text also points to the high-priestly ministry of Jesus as another provision of assurance. His priesthood is after the order of Melchizedek. It is a priesthood that is never-failing, never-ending. He is forever living and watching over the covenantal promises. The priest exists to repair damages to the covenant caused by our failures. He is the intercessor who shields us from the judgements of God and keeps divine favor over our lives.

As a result of His promises, His oath, His Blood and His priestly ministry, we have our HOPE anchored in Christ.

Hope is expectation. Our expectations are sure to manifest. It means that when we pray, when we make declarations, our faith is to be firmly placed in the promises of God. We must be assured beyond a shadow of a doubt that God will honor His word. God will provide, God will protect, God will defend, God will deliver, God will heal.

In addition, the passage shows that we operate behind the curtain. Behind the curtain in the Tabernacle of Moses is the place where the Mercy Seat is. This is a 'type' of the Throne of God. We operate from the place of the Throne. Inside that box are: The Ten Commandments, a pot of manna and also the rod of Aaron. The rod speaks of spiritual authority; manna is the revelation knowledge of God; and the tablets with the covenant—they were chiseled into stones shaped like hearts, indicating that functioning at that place effectively requires a heart of love for God and an above-average commitment to obey and honor Him. The intercessor, under the New Covenant, is not praying from the place of Altars, but a place of Thrones. This 'Royal Dimension' is praying from the place of complete transformation of life, spiritual authority and specific revelation regarding the prevailing circumstances into which he is speaking.

Prayer

My Heavenly Father, I thank you for the many things that you have revealed to me, especially in the area of prayer. Based upon the integrity of your Word, I boldly proclaim that I am redeemed from all my sins and I stand in the righteousness of God. You promised me sonship, therefore, I am of the stock of God. You promised me precision guidance, so I shall accurately make all decisions. You promised me success, so I declare I am successful in all of my doings. You promised me prosperity, and so I declare that I am abundantly supplied, and millions of dollars are in my domain. I have houses and lands and sufficient money to bless three generations. You promised me a saved family. So, I declare that all of my children will walk in the ways of God and shall do your perfect will. My wife is a happy and blessed woman.

I will not relent and will not retreat. I will not meander in the maze of mediocrity. I will not hesitate in the face of adversity nor shrink back from challenges. I defeat every satanic foe and overcome every human resistance to my progress. I declare that the works of my hands are successful, and my assets are secure. These things I speak in Jesus' name, Amen.

NOTES

> "PRAYER AT THE 'ALTAR DIMENSION' DEPICTS PRAYER AT ITS MOST BASIC LEVEL. IT IS FOUNDATIONAL."

CHAPTER 5

Altars – Foundations for Effective Prayer

Our case put forward thus far, is that prayer at the Altar Dimension depicts prayer at its most basic level. It encapsulates a consciousness of sins forgiven, the promises of God, and essential principles that govern receiving favorable responses from Heaven. Central to this level, as well, is the issue of how we physically position our bodies when we are praying. Because the majority of people are not successful intercessors, they ignore the significance of posturing the body.

The way we position the body in prayer may seem insignificant, but when we hit the realm of major accomplishments, we will note that it is not. A careful review of people in the Bible whose prayer broke through into major achievements and uncommon discoveries, we note that they changed the way they prayed as far as body posture is concerned. I think, in the heavens, it adds volume to our prayer and amplifies the requests of the soul. I believe we communicate verbally and non-verbally, even to God, and not just to each other.

If a person comes up to you in the street and stretches out the hand with the palm facing upward, we instantly know that they are begging for something. If a man goes within distance of a police officer and points his index finger to the officer and then jerks it back and upward, he is indicating that he would like to shoot the officer. Trouble is most likely to follow this scenario. Notice that when in agony or anguish of soul, a person may fold up into the fetal position. In this posture, the person subconsciously attempts to return to the place of greatest security in their life: that is, the womb of a mother. The hanging head may imply shame. I have heard that when a person sleeps on their back, it indicates complete security and courage.

We now enter the world of body language in relation to intercession. Most agree that we send off requests and emotions by the way we position the body. If one tilts their head, it may be to indicate that they are listening, or that they are trying to hear more clearly what is being said. A man is said to be attracted to a young lady if he looks her in the eyes, then at her lips, and then at her eyes again. They call this the 'flirting triangle'. It may truly mean that he is interested in her. During sex, one position may afford a deeper sense of gratification or expression than others.

Any alert person can read another person like a book. By your body posture, one may be able to tell that you are new in the area, or that you are stranded. Someone may be able to identify whether you are sophisticated or not, just by looking at you. Your body can send out a signal that you are looking for love "tonight." Your body posture can say that you are interested, or you are not. Notice that in all these scenarios, not a word is spoken; without a word the message is sent, the experience told, the emotions expressed.

I would dare to say that because the Holy Spirit thought it significant enough to mention prayer postures in the Bible, we should somehow take note of them. As we stretch forth our hearts and minds, we are learning more and more about the spirit world and how to interact with it successfully. Perhaps we will have to change how we view the mind of God on this matter. He thinks that it is important. God takes this so seriously that He set a prohibition on bowing before false gods.

> *[4] "You shall not make for yourself an image [idol] in the form of anything in heaven above or on the earth beneath or in the waters below. [5]* **You shall not bow down to them or worship them**; *for I, the Lord your God, am a jealous God..." (Exodus 20:4-5a - NIV - Emphasis Added)*

Note the following observations:

1) Making an idol, and bowing down to them, are treated by God as two different things.

2) Bowing down to them is positioning your body intentionally before them; and this

is a serious matter to God. It indicates a respect for them that is sinful.

3) God is offended by our participation in these activities because He is a jealous God. The way you position yourself next to an idol indicates a love for it, or an expectation of receiving something of value from it—revealing a reverence and esteem for a man-made deity which only God is worthy of.

Successful intercessors have all used various postures when praying. We will look at a number of them and see the incredible significance they bring.

A. Lying Prostrate Before the Lord

This position is incredibly powerful. We see a few instances of this in the Bible and it seems to have very deep spiritual significance. Firstly, it is an extreme expression of 'unworthiness'. It elevates the uniqueness and perfection of God in our hearts to sublime levels.

Abraham, the man of prayer, was completely shocked when God initiated a 'blood covenant' with him. Because blood-covenanting was a familiar practice in Abraham's time, he knew exactly what God was saying when He instituted this divine pact. For God to cut a covenant with him meant that all God had was his, and all he had was God's. His enemies were now God's enemies, and he was now a 'Partner in Purpose' with God. This covenant took on deep implication: it was as if he was now married to God and his surname was now 'God'. This is the reason that God referred to Himself as "the God of Abraham." Upon realizing this, Abraham fell on his face in awe because, I'm sure, he could not imagine that the God of the Universe would choose him—a man with a pagan background—and desire to bless him to such an extent. His falling prostrate before God was to acknowledge the majesty of God, and his own unworthiness of God's favor.

> *¹ When Abram was ninety-nine years old, the Lord appeared to him and said, "I am God Almighty; walk before me faithfully and be blameless. ² Then I will make my covenant between me and you and will greatly increase your numbers."*
>
> *³ **Abram fell facedown**, and God said to him, ⁴ "As for me, this is my covenant with you: You will be the father of many nations. ⁵ No longer will you be called Abram; your name will be Abraham, for I have made you a father of many nations. ⁶ I will make you very fruitful; I will make nations of you, and kings will come from you. ⁷ I will establish my covenant as an everlasting covenant between me and you and your descendants after you for the generations to come, to be your God and the God of your descendants after you. ⁸ The whole land of Canaan, where you now reside as a foreigner, I will give as an everlasting possession to you and your descendants after you; and I will be their God."*
>
> *⁹ Then God said to Abraham, "As for you, you must keep my covenant, you and your descendants*

after you for the generations to come. ¹⁰ This is my covenant with you and your descendants after you, the covenant you are to keep: Every male among you shall be circumcised. ¹¹ You are to undergo circumcision, and it will be the sign of the covenant between me and you. ¹² For the generations to come every male among you who is eight days old must be circumcised, including those born in your household or bought with money from a foreigner—those who are not your offspring. ¹³ Whether born in your household or bought with your money, they must be circumcised. My covenant in your flesh is to be an everlasting covenant. ¹⁴ Any uncircumcised male, who has not been circumcised in the flesh, will be cut off from his people; he has broken my covenant." (Genesis 17:1-14 - NIV - Emphasis Added)

Falling prostrate before God was also done when there was extreme crisis on a national or communal scale.

² Now there was no water for the community, and the people gathered in opposition to Moses and Aaron. ³ They quarreled with Moses and said, "If only we had died when our brothers fell dead before the Lord! ⁴ Why did you bring the Lord's community into this wilderness, that we and our livestock should die here? ⁵ Why did you bring us up out of Egypt to this terrible place? It has no grain or figs, grapevines or pomegranates. And there is no water to drink!" ⁶ Moses and Aaron went from the assembly to the entrance to the Tent of Meeting and **fell facedown,**

and the glory of the Lord appeared to them. ⁷ The Lord said to Moses, ⁸ "Take the staff, and you and your brother Aaron gather the assembly together. Speak to that rock before their eyes and it will pour out its water. You will bring water out of the rock for the community so they and their livestock can drink."
(Numbers 20:2-8 - NIV - Emphasis Added)

This was a serious matter, not only because the lack of water threatened the lives of hundreds of thousands of people, but they were also on the verge of losing faith in God and in the mission of Moses. The situation was grave and needed urgent divine intervention. Realizing this, the leadership went to the edge of the Tabernacle where God's presence resided and **fell prostrate** and prayed. **God responded** with a national miracle.

B. Kneeling

Perhaps kneeling is the most known prayer posture in the world. Kneeling empowers the position of a person's spirit that they have surrendered to the Sovereignty or Lordship of Christ and are willing to live in obedience to His Word. Note as well, that the bowing of the head and kneeling are treated as two different postures. The bending of the knee is indicative of a surrendered walk (changed life).

> *⁹ Therefore God exalted him to the highest place and gave him the name that is above every name, ¹⁰ that at the name of Jesus* **every knee should bow**, *in heaven and on earth and under the earth, ¹¹ and*

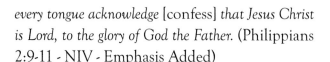

every tongue acknowledge [confess] that Jesus Christ is Lord, to the glory of God the Father. (Philippians 2:9-11 - NIV - Emphasis Added)

Kneeling is a powerful expression of humility.

C. Standing

Hear the words of the great Elijah the Tishbite:

¹ And Elijah the Tishbite, who was of the inhabitants of Gilead, said unto Ahab, As the Lord God of Israel liveth, **before whom I stand***, there shall not be dew nor rain these years, but according to my word.* (1 Kings 17:1 - KJV)

These words were repeated several times in the life of Elijah. They describe a basic posture he would be in when he prayed. They also imply that he was a man of frequent prayer and describes the spiritual platform of his daily life. He would stand before God, and so, challenged anything that was out of divine purpose from that place of prayer. As a prelude to challenging worldly systems, he would say, "the God before whom I stand..."

'Standing' before the Lord indicates a readiness to contend with all of the enemies of God within your jurisdiction. Paul says,

¹⁰ Finally, be strong in the Lord and in his mighty power. ¹¹ Put on the full armor of God so that you can take your stand against the devil's schemes. ¹² For our struggle is not against flesh and blood, but against the

rulers, against the authorities, against the powers of this dark world and against the spiritual forces of evil in the heavenly realms. ¹³ *Therefore put on the full armor of God, so that when the day of evil comes, you may be able to stand your ground, and after you have done everything,* **to stand**. ¹⁴ **Stand firm** *then, with the belt of truth buckled around your waist, with the breastplate of righteousness in place,* ¹⁵ *and with your feet fitted with the readiness that comes from the gospel of peace.* ¹⁶ *In addition to all this, take up the shield of faith, with which you can extinguish all the flaming arrows of the evil one* ¹⁷ *Take the helmet of salvation and the sword of the Spirit, which is the word of God.* ¹⁸ *And pray in the Spirit on all occasions with all kinds of prayers and requests. With this in mind, be alert and always keep on praying for all the Lord's people.* (Ephesians 6:10-18 - NIV - Emphasis Added)

It is interesting that it is in the context of spiritual warfare, that the Apostle speaks of standing before the Lord.

Standing before the Lord indicates acute awareness of one's relationship with God. It speaks to the intercessor's God-Consciousness. He is aware of who he is in God and of the finished work of Christ at Calvary that provides the basis of boldness. I think it necessary to establish this fact with some specificity. Each intercessor must put on his badge of rank. He must know who he is within the economy of the Kingdom of God. Again, there are some basic elements that should be at the forefront of our minds: We are not what we were, for in Christ our old self perished. Look at a glorious description of our blood-washed transformation:

> **CRUCIFIED:** ⁶ For we know that **our old self was crucified with him** so that the body ruled by sin might be done away with. (Romans 6:6a - NIV)
>
> **DEAD:** ⁸ Now if **we died with Christ**, we believe that we will also live with him. (Romans 6:8 - NIV)
>
> **BURIED:** ⁴ We were therefore **buried with him** through baptism. (Romans 6:4a - NIV)
>
> **RAISED:** ¹ Since, then, **you have been raised with Christ**, set your hearts on things above, where Christ is seated at the right hand of God. (Colossians 3:1 - NIV)
>
> **ASCENDED:** ⁶ And **God raised us up with Christ** and seated us with him in the heavenly realms in Christ Jesus. (Ephesians 2:6 - NIV)

And so, we are Foreknown, Predestined, Chosen and Reconciled:

> **FOREKNOWN:** ²⁹ For **whom He foreknew**, He also predestined to be conformed to the image of His Son, that He might be the firstborn among many brethren. (Romans 8:29 - NKJV)
>
> **CHOSEN:** ⁴ Coming to Him as to a living stone, rejected indeed by men, but **chosen by God** and precious. (1 Peter 2:4 - NKJV)

PREDESTINED: ¹¹ In Him also we have obtained an inheritance, **being predestined** according to the purpose of Him who works all things according to the counsel of His will. (Ephesians 1:11 - NKJV)

WE ARE GIVEN UNHINDERED ACCESS: ¹⁸ For through Him we both **have access** by one Spirit to the Father. (Ephesians 2:18 - NKJV)

SONS OF GOD: ² Beloved, now **we are sons of God**." (1 John 3:2 - NKJV)

A NEW SPECIES OF BEING: ¹⁷ Therefore, if anyone is in Christ, **he is a new creation**. (2 Corinthians 5:17a - NKJV)

WE ARE HEIRS OF THE KINGDOM: ⁷ Therefore you are no longer a slave but a son, and if a son, then **an heir of God through Christ**. (Galatians 4:7 - NKJV)

WE HAVE BEEN ACQUITTED OF SIN: ¹ Therefore, **having been justified** by faith, we have peace with God through our Lord Jesus Christ. (Romans 5:1 - NKJV)

WE STAND GUILTLESS: ⁸...that I may gain Christ ⁹ and be found in Him, not having my own **righteousness,** which is from the law, but that **which is through faith in Christ**. (Philippians 3:8b,9 - NKJV)

SANCTIFIED: ³⁰...Christ Jesus, who became for us...**sanctification**. (1 Corinthians 1:30b - NKJV)

WE HAVE BEEN MADE PERFECT IN HIM: ¹⁴ For by one sacrifice **he has made perfect forever** those who are being made holy. (Hebrews 10:14 - NIV)

WE ARE HIS POSSESSION: ¹⁴ who is a deposit guaranteeing our inheritance until the redemption of those who are **God's possession**. (Ephesians 1:14 - NIV)

WE ARE INDWELT AND SEALED: ¹³...having believed, **you were sealed with the Holy Spirit of promise**, ¹⁴ who is the guarantee of our inheritance... (Ephesians 1:13b-14a - NKJV)

We needed to establish the basis of our 'standing' before the God of Heaven. This is who we are. *He* has brought us near to Him by His grace. Standing before Him is embodied in all of these components. Elijah-under the Old Covenant-took the liberty to 'stand' before God, however, *we* who have been washed in the blood of Jesus are even *more* qualified to have boldness and power to 'stand' in the presence of our God.

D. Upraised Hands

Interestingly, the lifting of the hands is also a New Testament concept. It is a most beautiful image of one's dependency on

God. Without uttering a word, the intercessor signals that he is completely dependent on God's grace and blessing for his daily life. It says that he is trusting God with, and for, his life. The upraised hands convince the soul, and convey to God, that He is the source of everything.

Speaking to this matter, the Apostle Paul said to Timothy:

> *¹ I urge, then, first of all, that petitions, prayers, intercession and thanksgiving be made for all people– ² for kings and all those in authority, that we may live peaceful and quiet lives in all godliness and holiness. ³ This is good, and pleases God our Savior, ⁴ who wants all people to be saved and to come to a knowledge of the truth. ⁵ For there is one God and one mediator between God and mankind, the man Christ Jesus, ⁶ who gave himself as a ransom for all people. This has now been witnessed to at the proper time. ⁷ And for this purpose I was appointed a herald and an apostle–I am telling the truth, I am not lying–and a true and faithful teacher of the Gentiles. ⁸ Therefore I want the men everywhere to pray, lifting up holy hands without anger or disputing.* (1 Timothy 2:1-8 - NIV)

He urges men to pray prayers for mass impact (everyone) and prayers for Governmental control and restraint upon civil leadership in a country. These are incredible concepts that speak to the unlimited power of prayer. These prayers include entreaties that control cultural nuances (lead a life of godliness) and war (lead a quiet and peaceable life). Paul the Apostle is saying that the prayers of the Church can stop wars, civil unrest or civil disobedience. It can restrain leaders, thus, stopping dictatorial tendencies. Dictatorships prevail in nations where people do not know how to pray.

Then Paul tells Timothy to mobilize the people into mass gatherings for the purpose of prayer. When they gather, Paul advises that in the company of many, the people should lift their hands towards the heavens and pray these awesome prayers. When taking up the posture of lifted hands, they demonstrate that God is their source on a personal level. When done in the open and amongst many, it indicates that God is the source of life for the nation.

E. Prayer Walking

The expression 'prayer walking' is not found in the Bible. I read about sixteen versions of the Bible and have not found the term anywhere in the Word of God. The various inferences we find, however, lend themselves to us concluding that 'prayer walking' or 'walking while praying' is a prophetic concept. This means that it is done only upon the directive of the Holy Spirit. The second aspect to it is that it is used as a lethal weapon of conquest and spiritual take over. It seems to generate a marching sound of the Armies of God and instill fear in the camp of the enemy.

The Lord directed Abraham to walk through the land as a strategy for taking it over. There was to be no war, no bloody revolution. Just the incredible wisdom and power of God.

> [14] *The Lord said to Abram after Lot had parted from him, "Look around from where you are, to the*

north and south, to the east and west. ¹⁵ All the land that you see I will give to you and your offspring forever. ¹⁶ I will make your offspring like the dust of the earth, so that if anyone could count the dust, then your offspring could be counted. ¹⁷ Go, **walk through the length and breadth of the land**, for I am giving it to you." (Genesis 13:14-17 - NIV - Emphasis Added)

I would not think that Abraham would walk about the land shopping or visiting neighbors and friends. It is a prophetic prayer strategy, because God told him to "walk through the land." He must have been in close dialogue and communion with the Father. He obviously kept his ears upon the lips of God for continued guidance and strategy.

If this strategy was unique to Abraham's journey, then God would not venture to also give it to Joshua. However, in the book of Joshua, we see the same dynamics.

> ¹ After the death of Moses the servant of the Lord, the Lord said to Joshua son of Nun, Moses' aide: ² "Moses my servant is dead. Now then, you and all these people, get ready to cross the Jordan River into the land I am about to give to them—to the Israelites. ³ **I will give you every place where you set your foot**, as I promised Moses. ⁴ Your territory will extend from the desert to Lebanon, and from the great river, the Euphrates—all the Hittite country—to the Mediterranean Sea in the west. ⁵ No one will be able to stand up against you all the days of your life.

> *As I was with Moses, so I will be with you; I will never leave you nor forsake you.* (Joshua 1:1-5 - NIV - Emphasis Added)

God promised Joshua that He would give him every place he set his foot upon—in other words—wherever he walked. This strategy is used to conquer territories and regions. Again, I believe that God causes the sound of the walking of the righteous to resound in the world of evil spirits. Indeed, our God is the God of Armies. He is the Lord of War. He is Jehovah Gibbor, the Mighty Warrior. Prayer walking is tantamount to warfare prayer. It attacks the spirits that have lingered and controlled cultures and Governmental systems for decades.

'Walking' in the Bible denotes 'lifestyle'. By extension, walking symbolizes the values and convictions of any society. We are told to "walk in the Spirit," "walk in love," and "walk uprightly," so we see the spiritual significance. We also know that the steps of a good man are ordered by the Lord. I believe that when we intentionally pray and walk through a nation, we are shaking the philosophical foundations of the place. We indicate to the spirits that a new kingdom is about to take over the region.

The taking of Jericho now makes all the sense in the world. Marching (or walking forcefully) was a divine strategy used to conquer this fortified city.

> *[1] Now Jericho was tightly shut because of the sons of Israel; no one went out and no one came in. [2] The Lord said to Joshua, "See, I have given Jericho into*

your hand, with its king and the valiant warriors. ³ You shall march around the city, all the men of war circling the city once. You shall do so for six days. ⁴ Also seven priests shall carry seven trumpets of rams' horns before the ark; then on the seventh day you shall march around the city seven times, and the priests shall blow the trumpets. ⁵ It shall be that when they make a long blast with the ram's horn, and when you hear the sound of the trumpet, all the people shall shout with a great shout; and the wall of the city will fall down flat, and the people will go up every man straight ahead." (Joshua 6:1-5 - NASB)

The gates of the city were tightly shut. This means that no one was allowed to go in or come out. This is not just a physical matter; this was the activity of Jericho's jurisprudence. This was the LAW. It was the position of the Governmental System of the city. They did not want the intermingling of the people of God because they feared that their satanic culture would fall. Their walls were not just a physical wall; they were mental and spiritual positions.

Observe the phrase used: "the wall of the city will fall down flat," in other words: collapse. We can extrapolate on the concept of collapsing walls. All the walls of that city collapsed by the prophetic walking of the people of God. Their established values with regard to business, money, marriage, law and politics; their walls of parenting and entertainment; perished at the sound of a marching, shouting company.

F. Birthing

The 'birthing position' may be one of the most powerful postures when in prayer. We find it in the prayer life of Elijah, the prophetic intercessor.

> *⁴¹ And Elijah said to Ahab, "Go, eat and drink, for there is the sound of a heavy rain." ⁴² So Ahab went off to eat and drink, but Elijah climbed to the top of Carmel, bent down to the ground and put his face between his knees. ⁴³ "Go and look toward the sea," he told his servant. And he went up and looked. "There is nothing there," he said. Seven times Elijah said, "Go back." ⁴⁴ The seventh time the servant reported, "A cloud as small as a man's hand is rising from the sea." So Elijah said, "Go and tell Ahab, 'Hitch up your chariot and go down before the rain stops you.'" ⁴⁵ Meanwhile, the sky grew black with clouds, the wind rose, a heavy rain started falling and Ahab rode off to Jezreel. ⁴⁶ The power of the Lord came upon Elijah and, tucking his cloak into his belt, he ran ahead of Ahab all the way to Jezreel.*
> (1 Kings 18:41-46 - NIV)

Elijah had declared a famine on the land. In an agrarian society, agriculture is the basis of the economy and the chief force behind the Gross Domestic Product. To declare a famine, is to incite an economic downturn. Famines and droughts in the Bible speak of recessions. This man of God issued a prophetic word that halted production in the entire nation for three and a half years. This is utterly amazing.

To reverse this recession and create an economic boom, Elijah had to do more than utter a prophetic word. When it was time to produce the miracle, the prophet of God went up to mount Carmel. The word 'Carmel' means 'fruitful, abundant and productive'. This would be quite a significant place of symbolism for the prophet to pray for God to prosper the nation again.

The position Elijah took on—bending with his head between his knees—is the posture some ancient women would adopt when they were giving birth to a baby. I think that this is a significant revelation when it comes to effective prayer. There are many prayer postures in the Bible—many ways people placed their bodies—but this man of God thought it needful to move into a birthing position to release a miracle of this magnitude. There was a famine in the Land for three and a half years. As we learnt, this was a recession of epic proportions. Yet in one powerful moment this man of God reversed it. Here is how the Apostle James describes it.

> [17] *Elijah was a human being, even as we are.* **He prayed earnestly** *that it would not rain, and it did not rain on the land for three and a half years.* [18] *Again he prayed, and the heavens gave rain, and the earth produced its crops.* (James 5:17-18 - NIV - Emphasis Added)

Although James does not point directly to the posture of Elijah's body, he uses the word that implies deep passion and travail as that of a woman in child-birth. He, the prophet, prayed **earnestly.** In this passage, James is using Elijah as an example of a person who prays with tremendous fervor. The King James Version of the Bible puts it this way:

> [16b] ...*The effectual* **fervent** *prayer of a righteous man availeth much.* (James 5:16b - KJV)

Elijah's body was folded into the birthing position, and this impassioned posture caught the attention of God; and the Lord responded with a national miracle. Sometimes it may be necessary to let the posture of our body speak of the request of our spirit. You and I can give birth to miracles of this sort. Elijah is said to be a man of like passions. This means that God would honor you as well when you are in your birthing position.

G. Leaning on a Prophetic Object

> [21] *By faith Jacob, when he was dying, blessed each of Joseph's sons, and worshiped as* **he leaned on the top of his staff.** (Hebrews 11:21 - NIV)

The fact that the Spirit of God thought it important enough to mention Jacob leaning upon his staff, there *must* be some significance to it. Often, some things are injected within the pages of the Bible that can be viewed as having no significance or relevance, but when we take a closer look, we find it is loaded with meaning. An example of this is the 'Prayer of Jabez'. Whilst the writer of the Chronicles was enumerating a long genealogical list of the descendants of Judah, the name 'Jabez' pops up.

> [10] *Jabez cried out to the God of Israel, "Oh, that you would bless me and enlarge my territory! Let your hand*

be with me, and keep me from harm so that I will be free from pain." **And God granted his request.** (1 Chronicles 4:10 - NIV - Emphasis Added)

This man was just injected into the pages of redemptive history in the midst of all his ancestors, and his noteworthiness could have easily been missed, but he prayed a prayer that has proven to be loaded with power and relevance to them who are suffering, even today.

It is a similar case with the passage recording Jacob worshipping while leaning on his staff. It can be taken for granted as being meaningless, but it is packed with potency. Jacob is now in his old age. He is probably physically weak and lame, yet his spirit was clearly potent. He is still in worship mode, understanding the force of prayer and worship in fulfilling the purposes of God.

Staffs in those days had carvings and marks on them as if they were battered and bruised from travelling for years. These days we see people with them, and they have these lovely carvings and markings done for style and fashion. This, however, was not the case of staff markings in ancient times. Staffs were used as a book. When things needed to be given significance, when things needed to be committed to memory or memorialized, travelers would use stones and knives to carve out the images and information of the events or data they needed to remember. It is quite possible that Jacob's staff was not any different.

On his staff must have been the record of how God gave him the birthright that was not his. On it must have been the record of the double portion blessing due to him because God not only gave him the position of the firstborn, but also the blessing. On this staff must have been the marks memorializing his encounter with God at Bethel, and the covenant which he had made to tithe to God of everything that he was blessed with. On this staff must have been the markings reminding him of how God prospered him in Laban's enterprises. He must have memorialized the favor God had shown to him when Esau spared his life and forgave him. He must have carved out markings to remind him of the wrestling match encounter he had with the heavenly being the night before he met Esau.

When Jacob leaned on his staff to pray and to worship God in his old age, he was expressing prophetic reliance upon the proven grace of God. There is no wonder that the account is mentioned in Hebrews 11, a chapter referred to as the Hall of Faith and the Hall of Fame. His prayers were done from a place of life and a heart of faith.

Jacob leaning upon his staff can be considered, what we may call, a 'prophetic act'. It may appear routine, but it possesses weighty spiritual significance. At times, we may be directed by the Holy Spirit to do something that is of far-reaching importance. Sometimes going into a child's room and praying in the bed may make an expression of faith necessary to signal Heaven of your heart's desire. Carrying a child's book bag while praying may invoke the force of faith to turn their focus around. One may be challenged with eviction from an apartment or a house. As you pray you may need to pick up the original letter of acceptance and pray with it. If in a divorce, one can go back to the place where the proposal was first agreed upon and pray there. I do not know why the Holy Spirit would mention these things, but these powerful acts of symbolism are recognized by God or He would not have mentioned them.

Please observe too that not one of these things were commanded by God. God simply responded favorably. Brethren, all of these postures were Spirit-led, and came from the passionate or desperate heart of people who earnestly sought the hand of God in their situations. You should also respond to the promptings of your spirit when you are seeking the face and the hand of God.

H. Head Upraised – Looking Upwards

[10] When the apostles returned, they reported to Jesus what they had done. Then he took them with him and they withdrew by themselves to a town called Bethsaida, [11] but the crowds learned about it and followed him. He welcomed them and spoke to them about the kingdom of God, and healed those who needed healing. [12] Late in the afternoon the Twelve came to him and said, "Send the crowd away so they can go to the surrounding villages and countryside and find food and lodging, because we are in a remote place here." [13] He replied, "You give them something to eat." They answered, "We have only five loaves of bread and two fish – unless we go and buy food for all this crowd." [14] (About five thousand men were there.)

But he said to his disciples, "Have them sit down in groups of about fifty each." ¹⁵ The disciples did so, and everybody sat down. ¹⁶ Taking the five loaves and the two fish and **looking up to heaven***, he gave thanks and broke them. Then he gave them to the disciples to distribute to the people. ¹⁷ They all ate and were satisfied, and the disciples picked up twelve basketfuls of broken pieces that were left over.* (Luke 9:10-17 - NIV - Emphasis Added)

This is an incredible story. In it we see the Lord Jesus—the ultimate intercessor—praying to multiply five loaves and two fish to feed thousands of people. The record shows that not only was the miracle accomplished and everyone satisfied, but that they ended up with plenty of left overs.

When Jesus prayed in this instance, the Word teaches that He took the meal in His hands and **LOOKED UP** towards Heaven. We may question the validity of the things we have taught in this chapter, but we cannot question the actions of our Lord. His prayer life was simply off the charts. He routed demons, broke barriers and enforced the will of God everywhere He went. Now we see Him 'looking up' physically when in prayer.

The context of this episode is mentioned to give value to the miracle. There was a crowd of people following the ministry of Jesus. They were now hungry. Then the Lord told the disciples to feed them. This, my friend, is a herculean task for many reasons:

1. **Too many to feed**. ¹⁴ (About five thousand men were there.) But he said to his disciples,

"Have them sit down in groups of about fifty each." (Luke 9:14 - NIV)

Now this count only took men into consideration. If we add the women and children, as they were there as well, this could easily reach to about fifteen thousand. The fact that they counted the people, indicates that someone was taking careful and factual account of the incident. We can deduct from this that there are times when reports and statistics factually indicate the true nature of a problem. But the lab report, the research and the science are not the end of the story. Heavenly intervention can change the outcome.

2. **Limited resources available.** [13b] "We have only five loaves of bread and two fish..." (Luke 9:13b)

3. **The time is too late to find a natural solution.** [12] **Late in the afternoon** the Twelve came to him and said, "Send the crowd away so they can go to the surrounding villages and countryside and find food and lodging, because we are in a remote place here." (Luke 9:12)

4. **The location is bad.** They were, according to the text, in a remote place. Out there in the wilderness there was no food; there was no opportunity; there was no alternative.

5. **No viable option.** The disciples said to the Lord, "send them away," (verse 12). Sometimes we are pressed into a corner where there is literally no viable option for a miracle. That, my friend, is when God steps in.

Our Lord took the bread and fish and then raised His head towards Heaven. His action indicated that the resources for His life were not coming from the earthly economic systems, nor the times and seasons of earth. His answers were not in the human analysis of stats and research. His source was that of His Father in Heaven. His raised head indicated that fact to those around Him, and was clearly honored by God.

As a boy, I recall the day when my mother came into the living room having put a pot of water on the little stove to cook to feed her hungry children, but there was no food in the house. She had been recently converted to the Lord Jesus Christ and found faith in Him, and she was learning to pray and believe God for answers to her prayer. With the burden of five famished little children sitting in that living room, she walked into the room where we were, lifted her hands and looked up to Heaven and called upon the name of the Lord. A few moments later people came knocking on the door and brought us chicken, rice, and vegetables and we all had a sumptuous meal that day. God had heard her cry and graciously responded.

It is my mother's faith that impacted me so deeply that it gave birth to my personal faith in God. It is this memorable moment that branded me on the inside and taught me as a child to look up to God as my heavenly source. It is that faith that took me around the world and raised me up to speak to millions of souls, lead thousands to the Lord in the born-again experience, funnel millions into the Kingdom, and deliver over five thousand personal prophecies worldwide. I cannot forget the tears streaming down my mother's black cheeks as she prayed earnestly while looking up to Heaven. So, I have learnt that though this was a physical act, it was a sign that my mother believed that God would supply her needs.

The psalmist David declared with the same dramatic posture of uplifted eyes, that God is his eternal source of help:

> *¹ I lift up my eyes to the hills—*
> *where does my help come from?*
> *² My help comes from the Lord,*
> *the Maker of heaven and earth.*
> *³ He will not let your foot slip—*
> *he who watches over you will not slumber;*
> *⁴ indeed, he who watches over Israel*
> *will neither slumber nor sleep.*
> *⁵ The Lord watches over you—*
> *the Lord is your shade at your right hand;*
> *⁶ the sun will not harm you by day,*
> *nor the moon by night.*
> *⁷ The Lord will keep you from all harm—*
> *he will watch over your life;*
> *⁸ the Lord will watch over your coming and going*
> *both now and forevermore.*
> (Psalm 121 - NIV)

Prayer

Heavenly Father, I commit myself to consistently partner with you for the accomplishment of divine objectives. I give myself entirely to you, leaving nothing behind. Sanctify me through and through with your Word and your Spirit, that I may stand blameless before you.

Grant me the grace to remove all inhibitions in my walk of holiness, wisdom and love. Help me to live from the place of a deep and abiding peace. I will saturate myself with the Word of God and nurture the deposit of the anointing thereby. Preserve me from evil and from the wicked one.

Preserve my name in the earth, that you may be glorified. Increase my righteousness and firmly fix my righteous

resolve. Increase my substance to millions of dollars. Increase my influence that others may come into a glorious relationship with Christ. Open doors of opportunity for ministry and for business. Grant me continued insight and revelational progress. Stretch forth your hand to perform signs, wonders and miracles in the name of your holy child Jesus. Make known your ways and your acts unto us. Revive your works in the midst of the people, and increase the number of them that believe by the millions in my city and in my nation. In Jesus' name, Amen.

> "WE SHOULD LEARN THE FUNDAMENTALS OF PRAYER AND MASTER THEM AS WE BECOME MORE MATURE IN OUR TIME WITH GOD."

CHAPTER 6

Principles for Effective Prayer

In this discourse, we would like to further remind ourselves that the New Testament does not bear a strong revelation of Altars. This is the philosophical platform upon which we are building this doctrine. What we find is a very strong position that the believer is seated with Christ in the heavenlies. He is required to function in life from this exalted place. The Altar Dimension of prayer defines the Church in its spiritual embryonic position. Because the Altar Dimension is **vital**, however, we do not abandon the concept, but **build** on it.

Advanced Spiritual Matters

Before we can enter that which is beyond the veil, we are to immerse ourselves in the foundational building blocks to effective prayer. God brings 'babies' into the Kingdom, however, He does not want us to remain at the 'baby stage', but to mature into full-grown 'sons'.

> ⁶ *For to us a child is born, to us a son is given, and the government will be on his shoulders...* (Isaiah 9:6a - NIV)

Note, the child is born, but the son is given the responsibility to be in charge of the empire. In the Kingdom of God, a child is not given governmental responsibility. Childhood speaks of immaturity and not necessarily age.

Spiritual Childhood is unstable, and driven by situations and not purpose.

> ¹³ *until we all reach unity in the faith and in the knowledge of the Son of God and become mature, attaining to the whole measure of the fullness of Christ.* ¹⁴ *Then we will no longer be infants, tossed back and forth by the waves, and blown here and there by every wind of teaching and by the cunning and craftiness of people in their deceitful scheming.* (Ephesians 4:13-14 - NIV)

One cannot rise to the heights of communion with God if we are driven by the happenings, like the waves of the sea. The mature one will not be shifting with the philosophies of people. He is mature, firmly committed to the eternal purposes of God, and so remains stable, strong, and sure. His prayers are enforcing the will of God within the context of the shifting fortunes of life.

This concept of an advanced, mature relationship with God is further expounded in *'W E Vine's Expository Dictionary* of *New Testament Words'*. Dr. Vine uses these two words ('Teknon' and 'Teknion') as synonyms, as they address the biological issues and facts of one's heredity. The value of these expressions is brought out in Romans 8:14-21. The Spirit bears witness with their spirit that they are "**children of God,**" and, as such, they are His heirs and joint-heirs with Christ. This stresses the fact of their spiritual birth (vv. 16,17). On the other hand, "as many as are **led** by the Spirit of God, these are **sons** of God," i.e., "these and no other." Their conduct gives evidence of the dignity of their relationship and their likeness to His character. The difference between the 'Teknon/Teknion' factor and us being called 'Children of God' has to do with operational maturity. In this same vein of thought, Paul argues that immaturity is a way of thinking; the way one arrives at conclusions.

> *⁹ For we know in part, and we prophesy in part, ¹⁰ But when that which is perfect comes, then that which is imperfect shall pass away. ¹¹ When I was a child, I spoke as a child, I understood as a child, I thought as a child. But when I became a man, I put away childish things.* (1 Corinthians 13:9-11 - MEV)

'Thinking' is the quality of your internal conversations. This is why Romans 8:14 indicates that the mature son is 'Spirit-led'—able to arrive at the same conclusions as the Holy Spirit. He thinks like God.

Paul went on to describe 'speaking' as one of the indicators of Childhood. This is not just to be understood in the realm of everyday talking; we can also apply this concept to prayer. So, when I was a child, I *prayed* as a child as well. When I took on manhood I learn to interact with the Father from the place of a spiritually mature son.

Then the Apostle said, "I **understood** as a child. But, when that which is perfect comes, **I put away the childish things.**" There is a point in which we are to speak the words of the mature in Christ and pray accurately as He did. We ought to have a changed vocabulary when we get before God. The same old prayer lingo will only get the results that it has been getting for years.

There is no wonder that the baptism of the Holy Spirit is designed to give us an improved way to pray. God's foundational concern is expressed here.

> *26 Likewise the Spirit also helpeth our infirmities: for we know not what we should pray for as we ought: but the Spirit itself maketh intercession for us with groanings which cannot be uttered. (Romans 8:26 - KJV)*

We do not always know what to pray for as we ought. This is not only referencing the 'prayer points' or the 'prayer subjects', but also the 'prayer strategy'. We are generally weak in this area. Romans 8:26 calls this an 'infirmity' or a 'weakness'.

The infilling of the Holy Spirit brings a new and improved way to pray. Under the New Covenant, God allows us to talk to Him supernaturally in the original language of Heaven. Understand that speaking in tongues was never designed for addressing one another. It was designed chiefly for speaking to God. This tongue bypasses all known and learnt earthly languages. Here are some "tongue-talking" facts to consider:

1. **When we speak in tongues, we are praying.**

   ² For anyone who speaks in a tongue does not speak to men but to God. Indeed, no one understands them; they utter mysteries by the Spirit. (1 Corinthians 14:2 - NIV)

   ¹⁴ For if I pray in an unknown tongue, my spirit prayeth, but my understanding is unfruitful. (1 Corinthians 14:14 - KJV)

2. **When we speak in tongues, we are speaking in a Heavenly Language.**

   ¹ᵇ ...I speak in the tongues of men **and of angels**... (1 Corinthians 13:1 - NIV)

3. **We should pray in the Spirit often.**

   ¹⁸ I thank God that I speak in tongues more than all of you. (1 Corinthians 14:18 - NIV)

4. **When we speak in tongues, we are bypassing our human limited intellect.**

   ¹⁴ For if I pray in an unknown tongue, **my spirit prayeth, but my understanding is unfruitful**. (1 Corinthians 14:14 - KJV)

5. **When we speak in tongues, we outwit the enemy on the battle fields of life.**

¹⁰ Finally, be strong in the Lord and in his mighty power. ¹¹ Put on the full armor of God so that you can take your stand against the devil's schemes. ¹² For our struggle is not against flesh and blood, but against the rulers, against the authorities, against the powers of this dark world and against the spiritual forces of evil in the heavenly realms. ¹³ Therefore put on the full armor of God, so that when the day of evil comes, you may be able to stand your ground, and after you have done everything, **to stand.** **¹⁴ Stand firm** *then, with the belt of truth buckled around your waist, with the breastplate of righteousness in place, ¹⁵ and with your feet fitted with the readiness that comes from the gospel of peace. ¹⁶ In addition to all this, take up the shield of faith, with which you can extinguish all the flaming arrows of the evil one. ¹⁷ Take the helmet of salvation and the sword of the Spirit, which is the word of God. ¹⁸ And* **pray in the Spirit** *on all occasions with all kinds of prayers and requests. With this in mind, be alert and always keep on praying for all the Lord's people.* (Ephesians 6:10-18 - NIV - Emphasis Added)

The Apostle Paul lists the issue of praying in the Spirit as the final piece of the armor of warfare. To be exegetically sound, you will note that he admonishes the believer to take up the armor: take the breastplate, the belt, the shield, the sword and the helmet. Then he comes to verse eighteen and says: ***"Pray in the Spirit."*** It can be understood like this: ***"Take up the weapons and go into prayer."*** The force of truth, faith, the rhema word, and the redemptive plan (gospel) are best utilized on the combat zone when we are praying in the Spirit.

I am convinced that when we step up in prayer, we must be stepping up on the fundamentals of prayer. There are basic principles to be learnt and practiced. However, most believers are strapped for years with the same tonality, same postures: (clasping of the hands and closing of the eyes) kind of prayer posturing. They are still praying with the same inflections and the same words. They have been stuck in this vein for dozens of years, without results.

We must now advance to a new place in our prayer life. Someone once said that an expert is one who masters the basics. So, we should learn the fundamentals of prayer and master them as we become more mature in our time with God.

Prayer must Address God the Father

This statement may seem simple, but it is profound. God does not mince words. He means what He says, and He says what He means. We may slight some statements in the Bible because we lack the understanding and/or the significance of them, or we may not like what it is saying to us. However, it was inserted into the 'Pages of Life' for a reason.

The context of the Lord's Prayer is this: Jesus' disciples were observing their Lord in prayer. They were so impressed with His way of talking to God, that they asked Him to teach them to pray as John the Baptist taught his disciples to pray. The fact that the Lord responded positively to their request means that one can be taught to pray. Therefore, we must conclude that there is a 'good' way and a 'not-so-good' way to pray. There is 'effective' intercession and 'ineffective' intercession. It implies that one can improve their prayer life.

Their request to be taught to pray like John taught, is not to say, "Teach us the same things that John taught his disciples." It can be concluded that they were implying: *"John had a school of prayer. Why don't you begin one too?"*

> *¹ [Jesus was] praying in a certain place; and when He stopped, one of His disciples said to Him, Lord, teach us to pray, [just] as John taught his disciples. ² And He said to them, When you pray,* **say: Our Father Who is in heaven**, *hallowed be Your name, Your kingdom come. Your will be done [held holy and revered] on earth as it is in heaven.* (Luke 11:1-2 - AMPC - Emphasis Added)

The first instruction the Lord gave His disciples as He began to teach them how to pray was: "When you pray, *address the FATHER.*"

> *²³* **In that day you will no longer ask me anything.** *Very truly I tell you,* **my Father** *will give you whatever you ask in my name.* (John 16:23 - NIV)

There are so many people who think that this point is insignificant, and one to be ignored. But God said it. The Master Teacher said it, therefore, it **has** to be of utmost importance. When the Lord prayed, He also—as an example—addressed the Father.

> *⁴¹So they took away the stone.* **Then Jesus looked up and said, "Father,** *I thank you that you have heard me. ⁴² I knew that you always hear me, but I said this for the benefit of the people standing here, that they may believe that you sent me."* (John 11:41-42 - NIV - Emphasis Added)

This is a most basic principle, and as we begin our journey, we should anchor our prayers on this. The object of our prayer is God, our Heavenly Father.

There are two aspects to the Fatherhood of God, however. I think that the most basic of the two is 'fatherhood' in the sense of 'care'. We can hold in strong faith that God the Father cares about us. He wants to meet all our needs and wants us to be abundantly supplied.

> *⁹ For you are becoming progressively acquainted with and recognizing more strongly and clearly the grace of our Lord Jesus Christ (His kindness, His gracious generosity, His undeserved favor and spiritual blessing), [in] that though He was [so very] rich, yet for your sakes He became [so very] poor, in order that by His poverty you might become enriched (abundantly supplied).* (2 Corinthians 8:9 - AMPC)

The other aspect of the Fatherhood of God goes beyond the economy of our needs; it speaks of 'genetic composition and relationship'. It means that we are of the stock of God. We belong to the 'God-breed'; the 'God-kind'. It is this realization that moves your prayers to another level of boldness and power. Here, your concept of sonship will change to not just having needs supplied, but becoming a builder of the Father's house, the Father's business, the family enterprise.

Prayer Should Begin with Worship

Our Lord told the Apostles to say, "Our Father who is in Heaven, *your name is hallowed*." Without dealing with the meaning of all these words, at the most basic level, worship prior to request is preferred in Heaven. Some people simply come to the Lord with a laundry list. Prayer, for them, is like going shopping. They make their shopping list and stroll the aisle of the supermarket, choosing and picking out the things they need. It is not that God does not want us to have those things, but as you build an effective prayer life, you need to know how to spend your time with Him.

Worship before request! Begin with gratitude. When I go to spend time with God, I begin by thanking Him for everything—and I list them. From good health, to my wife, kids, ministry, friends, home, cars, money; I mean I literally call names and numbers to Him. That practice has taught me to be grateful for the life that the Lord has given me.

⁴ **Enter his gates with thanksgiving** *and his courts with praise; give thanks to him and praise his name.* (Psalm 100:4 - NIV)

Then tell Him how awesome He is. This is most beautiful. At this point, honestly, my spirit moves to a place of brokenness. Just the awareness that God has allowed me to come close to Him in all His splendor and majesty is so super awesome, that, more than words can tell, I honor and revere His most holy and matchless name. It is my belief that each one of us should learn to start here. Spend quality time in adoration and admiration of the greatness of God. This sets the stage—not in the sense of deceiving or tricking God to meet your need—but it is the protocol to His presence and does bring a smile upon His face.

Prayer Should Be Developed on Continued Repentance

Our Lord told His disciples to say, "hallowed be your name." This elevates the essential characteristic of God as 'holy' or 'sinless'. We should see this in contrast to ourselves. As we begin to pray, we should acknowledge His redeeming grace. I am not suggesting that we should pray with guilt, shame and condemnation; I am saying we should acknowledge that, no matter how victorious we have lived, we are where we are by the grace of God, and that there is no man that does not sin.

Consequently, quality time in prayer should be spent in confession of sin. We should always go through a time of cleansing. The opposite of that would bring in a sense of arrogance and pride. These deadly enemies of faith and prayer should be avoided at all cost.

In this season, I have learnt that there are errors in our lives that we sometimes ignore or act as if they are unimportant. I would confess that I have made mistakes as a father. I confess that I have made dumb mistakes as a Pastor. I'll confess poor money management, or that I have not honored my word at times. My friend, time with God is an awesome privilege. We should not waste it nor play games with Him. He knows our thoughts, our motives, and our secret sins. There is no benefit in hiding it from Him. But there is tremendous power in confessing sins before Him. Saying "'Hallowed' be Thy Name," is not just to say, "I recognize Your holiness." It is to admit my sinfulness as well.

Prayer Must Be Made from A Consciousness of The Power of God

Our Lord taught His disciples to say, "Hallowed is your Name." The mention of the name of God is quite interesting and would probably take another book to teach it. But it speaks to an understanding of the Omnipotence of God. The name here is not plural. There is really only one sacred name for God to which the Lord must be referring.

Coded into the King James Bible is a mysterious insight into the name of God. Whenever the word 'God' is seen in the text with a capital 'G', the word 'Elohim' is usually the Hebrew equivalent. Whenever the word 'Lord', with a capital 'L' is seen, the word 'Adonai' is the Hebrew equivalent. However, whenever the words 'GOD' or 'LORD' appear in all caps, the Hebrew equivalent is the word 'Yahweh'. By presenting these three "names" for God in this way, we can assume that these words are of utmost importance. Still, the word 'Yahweh' takes it to another level.

I do not belong to the Assemblies of Yahweh, but I *do* believe that the name of God is 'Yahweh'. It is a sacred name for God held in the highest regard amongst the Jewish people. It is spelt "YHWH" in the original language. It is a word of four consonants called a 'tetragrammaton'. This is the word used when God told Moses "I AM that I AM."

> *¹³ Moses said to God, "Suppose I go to the Israelites and say to them, 'The God of your fathers has sent me to you,' and they ask me, 'What is his name?' Then what shall I tell them?" ¹⁴ God said to Moses, "I AM WHO I AM. This is what you are to say to the Israelites: 'I AM has sent me to you.'"* (Exodus 3:13-14 - NIV)

This word "YHWH", the "I AM", refers to God as the self-existent one. That statement is loaded. It means that He does not need anything to exist. This is a mind-blowing fact. God does not need an environment. He is bigger than the Universe. The 'Universe' or the 'multiverse' lives **in** Him. **By Him** all other things consist and have their existence. They need Him; He does not need them. He does not live in light nor darkness. He is not *in* anything, for nothing supports Him. God is absolute in every way. He does not grow; He does not learn. He is not moving (He is already there - Omnipresent). Also, He determines the form of His own existence. He could manifest like a bird, a man, a cloud, wind, fire... anything whatsoever. There is no limit to the form He can take on.

He is absolute in power. There is literally nothing that is too hard for God. Nothing is impossible with Him.

> [17] Ah Lord God! behold, thou hast made the heaven and the earth by thy great power and stretched out arm, and **there is nothing too hard for thee**: (Jeremiah 32:17 - KJV - Emphasis Added)

Our prayers should always be made from the standpoint of the mighty power of God. This is what the Lord was teaching the disciples. This would mean that we should never be discouraged or intimidated with the size of our need or the nature of the problem. When you step into prayer, you step into the realm of YAHWEH. You step into the world of infinite possibilities.

The Apostle Paul strengthens this argument in the book of Ephesians

> [20] Now to Him Who, by (in consequence of) the [action of His] power that is at work within us, is able to [carry out His purpose and] do superabundantly, far over and above all that we [dare] ask or think [infinitely beyond our highest prayers, desires, thoughts, hopes, or dreams]– [21] To Him be glory in the church and in Christ Jesus throughout all generations forever and ever. Amen (so be it). (Ephesians 3:20-21 - AMPC)

Prayer Must Be Made in Jesus' Name

Though not mentioned in the Lord's prayer, Jesus Himself taught us that we should pray in His name. We should also use the name of the Lord Jesus as a key. It provides the legal basis for our prayers. Here is how the Lord puts it:

> *²³ In that day you will no longer ask me anything. Very truly I tell you, my Father will give you* **whatever you ask in my name**. *²⁴ Until now you have not asked for anything in my name. Ask and you will receive, and your joy will be complete.* (John 16:23-24 - NIV - Emphasis Added)

There may be layers of truth embedded in this statement, but on the surface, we are motivated to breathe this holy name in prayer. Not only is this doctrinally correct, but we see how the disciples used it when they prayed. They must have understood what Jesus was saying as they walked closely with Him.

> *⁴ Peter looked straight at him, as did John. Then Peter said, "Look at us!" ⁵ So the man gave them his attention, expecting to get something from them. ⁶Then Peter said, "Silver or gold I do not have, but what I do have I give you.* **In the name of Jesus Christ of Nazareth, walk**.*"* (Acts 3:4-6 - NIV - Emphasis Added)

When they prayed, they uttered the name of Jesus as an access strategy. His name gets God's attention. His name invokes the terms of the New Covenant as provided through the shed blood of Christ at Calvary.

Indeed, there is power in that Name. Notice what the Apostle Paul says about this.

> *⁹ Therefore God also has highly exalted Him and given Him the name which is above every name, ¹⁰ that at the name of Jesus every knee should bow, of those in heaven, and of those on earth, and of those under the earth, ¹¹ and that every tongue should confess that Jesus Christ is Lord, to the glory of God the Father.* (Philippians 2:9-11 - NKJV)

Paul is teaching in this text, that at the use or the sound of this Name, **beings bow in Heaven**. 'Bowing' here, I am convinced, refers not only to the bending of the knee, but also to responding favorably. At this Name, Heaven stands ready to respond. This, and I say this cautiously, includes the Father and all of the Angelic Hosts.

Then Paul says that at the name of Jesus every knee shall bow, of beings **under the earth**... Under the earth? He is talking about the kingdom of Satan. "Under the earth" refers to every demon and also all them that are dead. Through this Name, one can command demonic spirits and they must respond accordingly.

At this Name—the name of Jesus—the entire kingdom of Satan must yield. Satan and his band of cohorts may terrorize unsuspecting humanity with evil, death and destruction, but once we, the Body of Christ, realize that the name of Jesus is our badge of rank, and that demons are to completely submit to us, then the kingdom of Darkness would be in trouble. Master spirits, principalities and powers bow down immediately at the mention of that Name.

Prayer Must Be Made from a Forgiving Heart

The Lord Jesus made it a point to interject the principle of forgiveness as a foundational concern to answered prayer. We should never come to God to pray while we are holding other people's offenses against them. This is a cardinal principle. The fact is, that sin is the ultimate barrier between man and His God. Unless God pardons man of all his sin, he has nothing to stand on when praying. God's hand is not shortened that it cannot save, heal, deliver and all the good things we may require of Him. However, it is the sins of man that block up the power of God and restrain His hand from moving favorably on our behalf.

> [1] *Surely the arm of the Lord is not too short to save, nor his ear too dull to hear.* [2] *But your iniquities have separated you from your God; your sins have hidden his face from you, so that he will not hear.* (Isaiah 59:1-2 - NIV)

Our access to the Father is predicated upon Him forgiving us of our sins. It is the reason that the New Covenant was initiated, making allowance for our sins to be washed away by the blood of Jesus. The two main redemptive covenants of the Bible—namely: The Mosaic and the New Covenants—are built around an elaborate system that removes the impact of

God, not only on the sinner, but also on Heaven. Each of them carries:

1) A system of Laws
2) A priesthood
3) Sacrifices
4) A tabernacle; and
5) Promises

The entire book of Hebrews is devoted to these subjects. The New Covenant is treated as a better and more superior covenant, because we are only to observe one law, and it is the 'Law of Love'. There is one superior sacrifice, that is: Christ and His blood is the final price for all sins—past, present, and future. He is the embodiment of a superior priesthood. His is a priesthood after the eternal order of Melchizedek, and this New Covenant is based upon better promises. Additionally, we do not deal with an earthly sanctuary. Ours is the sanctuary of Heaven itself.

It is this profound and powerful system that establishes our redemption and forgiveness of sins. Through this powerful system, we have not only had our record in Heaven expunged and all evidence of sin removed from the archives of the Universe, but we too have been cleansed in our spirit from the involuntary production of sin and from the stain on our person that sin causes.

> [22] *let us draw near to God with a sincere heart and with the full assurance that faith brings, having our hearts sprinkled to cleanse us from a guilty conscience*

and having our bodies washed with pure water. ²³*Let us hold unswervingly to the hope we profess, for he who promised is faithful.* (Hebrews 10:22-23 - NIV)

Taking into account the major sacrifice Jesus made to cleanse us from sin, it is a serious evil to pray while keeping offense in our hearts. We cannot justifiably hold others in our hearts with evil intent. We simply cannot be unforgiving to others, regardless of the offense. God takes this seriously and will refuse to respond to our prayers.

²⁵*And when you stand praying, if you hold anything against anyone, forgive him, so that your Father in heaven may forgive you your sins."* (Mark 11:25 - NIV)

The Apostle Mark records this at a critical juncture. Our Lord was teaching the faith principle of changing the molecular structure of matter. "Speak to the mountain…" is the resounding declaration. In other words, "Speak to the inanimate Universe and alter its nature and relocate it to your preference." Have the faith of God, or faith *like* God has it.

Then He switches on another Prayer Dimension. The first is the prayer of decree and declaration: Speaking to things. Then He made an additional point: "When you stand praying or petitioning God—FORGIVE!" You should always do so from the inner place of a heart free of human offense. When we refuse to forgive others their offenses against us, we neutralize the construct of the New Covenant. We "tie" the hands of God. The priesthood of Jesus, the blood of the everlasting covenant, the sanctuary of Heaven, the eternal never-failing promises of God, are all suspended in our lives and the economy of prayer fails in our individual worlds. Heaven goes on pause when it is approached by an unforgiving heart.

The Lord Jesus also talked about this when teaching the disciples to pray. He noted this as of central concern to a strong life of prayer.

> *⁴ And forgive us our sins; for we also forgive every one that is indebted to us...* (Luke 11:4a - KJV)

In His earth walk, the Lord dealt with this problem in the hearts of His followers. He stressed it by indicating that both the regularity of the offense and the nature of the offense are to be overcome to allow the forgiveness of God to flow through us.

> *³² And become useful and helpful and kind to one another, tenderhearted (compassionate, understanding, loving-hearted), forgiving one another [readily and freely], as God in Christ forgave you.* (Ephesians 4:32 - AMPC)

In this passage, Paul addresses not just the humility of the heart in forgiving others, but the extent to which we are to forgive. We are told to forgive in the manner that Christ forgives. This has to do with the measure, the extent, to which we must go to forgive others.

> *²¹ Then came Peter to him, and said, Lord, how oft shall my brother sin against me, and I forgive him? till seven times? ²² Jesus saith unto him, I say not*

unto thee, Until seven times: but, Until seventy times seven. (Matthew 18:21-22 - KJV)

Note that this passage demonstrates the regularity with which we are to forgive others. The seventy times seven is regarded as if needed in one day. But God does not intend that we literally count, and so when we would have exhausted the number stated, that we stop forgiving. Seventy times seven is not just four hundred and eighty times in this instance, but rather, the absolute completeness of regular unlimited forgiveness.

Praying from a forgiven heart is needed to have power with God. I must emphasize this, because one cannot but see the incredibly powerful covenantal system set up in the Old and New Testaments so as to provide God the legal basis to acquit the guilty of sin. Hundreds of thousands of animals were slain under the Old Covenant. Countless people died attempting to execute the protocols to establish forgiveness within the community of God's people. Therefore, we should not take this lightly at all. This is no joking matter and it is not to be undertaken with levity of heart. Forgiving people of their offenses should be dealt with immediately and seriously.

Prayer Must Be Made in Accordance with The Will of God

There are other principles we must learn as foundational to a life of effective prayer, and we cannot be totally exhaustive in this book. But this point we must address: "Prayer is to be made in accordance with the will of God." Here are some scriptures that speak on this matter.

> ¹⁴ *This is the confidence we have in approaching God: that if we ask anything according to his will, he hears us.* ¹⁵ *And if we know that he hears us—whatever we ask—we know that we have what we asked of him.* (1 John 5:14-15 - NIV)

> ⁷ *If ye abide in me, and my words abide in you, ye shall ask what ye will, and it shall be done unto you.* (John 15:7 - KJV)

Now let me state here that asking according to the will of God has two specific dimensions to it:

1. **The request must have biblical reference.** Some time ago, I was in a rural area in St. Vincent and the Grenadines, and I was sitting in on a panel discussion on the subject: 'Love, Courtship and Marriage'. After presenting with the other two persons who were on the panel, the floor was opened for questions. A "smart" student stood and asked me, **"The Bible says** 'thou shalt not commit adultery.' What do **you** say?" If this inquiry was not such a serious misdemeanor on the part of the attendee, it would have been quite funny. But such a question should *never* be asked, especially after prefacing the question with *"The Bible says..."*

   This represents a blatant disregard for what God has already established as being His will on the matter.

We should not ask God to cause a person to die so we could have their wife or husband. This is because marriage already has strong biblical authority attached to it, and God would not override His Word to act according to this misdirected request. To pray effectively, we are to know the will of God. I am aware that many people in the Kingdom of God are cognizant of this, but I need to reiterate it as we lay the foundation for advanced levels of intercession. The intercessor is to arm himself adequately—not just with his needs or the needs of others. He is not just required to have statistics and reports at his disposal. Some have studied communities and mapped out areas of satanic activity and decoded the principalities operating in the area. Yet when they begin to pray, their prayers are out of line with the Father's plan, and so become just verbiage and empty sayings.

2. **There is a second and more telling understanding to praying in the will of God.** It is spoken of in St. John's Gospel.

⁷ If ye abide in me, and my words abide in you, ye shall ask what ye will, and it shall be done unto you. (John 15:7 - KJV)

This shifts the focus of the will of God from a theoretical, doctrinal or philosophical matter, to a **positional** concern. The Lord Jesus said, "If you abide **IN ME**...then you shall ask for what you want, and I will give it to you." The issue here is not necessarily quoting a verse to back up our requests, but, more importantly, that we are living in the plans and purposes of God; walking in a manner that pleases Him.

Hence, I can ask with boldness. I do not need a verse to tell me God wants me to have a helicopter. I just want it for a toy. I do not need a prophetic word saying that God wants me to have a ten-bedroom house. If I am in His will, He will give me what I want. This is why He speaks to the issue of my qualified desires.

24 Therefore I say unto you, What things soever ye desire, when ye pray, believe that ye receive them, and ye shall have them. (Mark 11:24 - KJV)

God did not make us robots. He gives us a free choice. We are free moral agents created by God Himself. God respects our desires, our preferences and our wants. Many of God's people are afraid to ask for things because they are afraid that they may ask outside of the will of God. Some misguided person may have told them that God only gives us our needs and not our wants. Or they may have said, "Do not ask for more than that which is necessary." This ideology glaringly contradicts Jesus' words granting us permission to make limitless requests— *"What things soever ye desire..."*

The Lord said this:

²⁴ Up to this time you have not asked a [single] thing in My Name [as presenting all that I AM]; but now ask and keep on asking and you will receive, so that your joy (gladness, delight) may be full and complete. (John 16:24 - AMPC)

"Ask," we are told—freely and boldly—and we will receive. The receiving here is acquiring something that you have never had before; or did not previously possess in an enhanced quantity or quality. Ask for things that you do not have or cannot attain through normal means or regular channels.

We are also admonished by our Lord to "Seek and you will find." 'Finding' speaks of the satisfied end of an adventure. It speaks of discovering the unknown. Seek for that which is hidden. This means that there is a dimension of prayer designed to make you the original at something; for example: make you an entrepreneur; or a great inventor or composer. The next hit song can be written by you. The next block buster movie can be yours. The next creative business idea can come from you. It is clear that the Lord was talking about the glorious adventure of discovery. Seek and you shall find.

Finally, He said, "Knock and the doors will be opened to you." Opened doors speak to the issue of 'access'. God wants you to access things that are inaccessible to masses. Prayer will make you gain entry to systems, people, organizations, and even countries. Faith will bring you into financial systems and spheres of authority that you have never had before. Do not let the spirit of failure and poverty intimidate you. Do not faint nor hesitate in the face of the enemy. Never meander in the maze of mediocrity or halt in the face of adversity. Enlarge your prayers and quicken your faith.

These viewpoints are foundational to an effective life of prayer. If you practice them, you will realize uncommon results. You will discover the hidden treasures of faith. They will be poured upon you in abundance. You are sure to enter a world of infinite possibilities and much more.

Prayer

Father in Heaven, your Word declares that we are blessed with all spiritual blessings in heavenly places, and I thank you for the riches of those blessings. Therefore, this is my creed. I believe and affirm that I am chosen of God. I believe that I am the righteousness of God in Christ Jesus. I believe that I am made in the image and likeness of God. I believe that I have the mind of Christ, and that I can do all things through Him who strengthens me. I believe that I am the seed of Abraham and, therefore, the heir of all the world's material blessing.

Because I am in Christ, God is in me and I am in God. I believe that the omniscience and omnipotence of God dwells in me. I have inexhaustible power, I have entrepreneurial power, I have defensive power, and the full authority to operate in the glory and the power of God.

Therefore, I cannot and will not fail, I will not be defeated, I will not be a victim of sinful habits and satanic invasions. My mind is strong, my body is strong, and my will is strong.

Now to Him Who, by (in consequence of) the [action of His] power that is at work within me, is able to carry out His purpose and do superabundantly, far over and above all that I can ask or think, infinitely beyond my highest prayers, desires, thoughts, hopes, or dreams, be praise and glory forever. In Jesus' name, Amen.

NOTES

> "THE CHURCH IS TO FUNCTION AS GOD'S 'LEGISLATIVE EXECUTIVE' IN THE SPIRIT, HAVING BEEN GIVEN KEYS TO BIND AND LOOSE."

CHAPTER 7

We are God's Legislative Executive

So far in our discourse—and I know that we may appear redundant—we are presenting on the premise that the New Testament does not focus specifically on the use of Altars. It is infrequent and almost non-existent that saints are viewed praying at Altars. Instead, we hear a call to come before the Throne, or you see the Church seated on the Throne with the Lord Jesus. Therefore, our language must change to the culture of royalty. Our prayers are to be configured differently. This is the philosophical platform upon which we are building this revelation. We will look more deeply into this fact.

The Church is called to function in a dimension of relationship with God that no other person or entity has. The place that the Church holds with God is unlike that of

Adam, Moses, Israel or even Abraham, God's friend. Paul puts it this way:

> *¹⁷ Therefore if any person is [ingrafted] in Christ (the Messiah) he is a new creation (a new creature altogether); the old [previous moral and spiritual condition] has passed away. Behold, the fresh and new has come!* (2 Corinthians 5:17 - AMPC)

This new 'ingrafted' position 'in Christ', launches us into an advantageous place that not even famed men of ancient biblical times were partakers of. This changes everything! including the way we are to talk to God, and the results we get. I am contending strongly that as the relationship with God has changed, so has our access to Heaven's resources and God's omnipotence changed.

At this juncture, the Church does not only pray upward to God, but the Church now legislates downward upon the material universe. The Church is not to ask God for things as a beggar or a pauper. We lay claim to, and command, as having all things available to us. We pray from the place of finished realities. Therefore, we are praying with decrees and declarations of faith. The Church functions in the Spirit as God's 'Legislative Executive', having been given keys to bind and loose.

> *¹⁷ Jesus replied, "Blessed are you, Simon son of Jonah, for this was not revealed to you by man, but by my Father in heaven. ¹⁸ And I tell you that you are Peter, and on this rock I will build* **my church**, *and the gates of Hades will not overcome it. ¹⁹* **I will give**

you the keys of the kingdom of heaven; whatever you bind on earth will be bound in heaven, *and* whatever you loose on earth will be loosed in heaven." (Matthew 16:17-19 - NIV - Emphasis Added)

In this text, the Lord Jesus, for the very first time in His ministry, for the very first time in redemptive history, and for the very first time in redemptive revelation, speaks of a body of people He calls 'the Church'. When He spoke of it, He immediately connects it to:

1) A Building Process - (On this rock I will build)
2) Prayer (Binding and Loosing)
3) The Kingdom of God
4) Keys (Speaking of complete and total access to the resources of the realm of God).

Because the Lord thought it so vitally important to use such language, we must then consider what the Church is.

It is interesting that Christ waited until He went to the region of Caesarea Philippi to initiate this "Church" discussion. The location must have influenced what He was thinking at the time. Phillip the tetrarch had rebuilt and beautified the city in honor of Tiberius Caesar, the reigning emperor. Viewing this context, the "building of the Church" discussion bears socio, economic and political implications. His initial use of the term was not religious at all.

The Greek word for 'Church' is the word 'Ekklesia', or sometimes spelt 'Ecclesia'. Its most early usage was by the principal assembly of the democracy of ancient Athens, therefore, a political term. The *Encyclopedia Britannica* describes it this way: "the gathering of those summoned." The *Encyclopedia* points to the fact that the term was used in the fifth and sixth century B.C. (Before Christ) to describe a gathering of select males over eighteen years old. They had FINAL authority in the city over the formulation of POLICY for the ways and means of the Governmental System of the city. *Britannica* indicates that assemblies of this sort existed in most Greek city-states and continued to function throughout the Hellenistic and Roman periods. A part of the responsibility of the Ekklesia was to appoint magistrates. Clearly then, the central function of the Church was to be a legislative executive. Under the Roman Empire, their powers gradually waned or weakened. It is in the face of this weakening of the powers of the Ekklesia that the Lord Jesus declared to a people that understood the historical significance of the Church, that He was about to build a new Church. In saying this, He established that He was a king and that a new Kingdom had come to take over the political systems of the day. Additionally, the body of people loyal to Him would now constitute the final authority of Policy for the city, and that they would be the ones appropriating the ways and means of the Government.

The Church of ancient times played the role of the Congress of the United States, the legislative branch of Government whose chief job it is to fund the Government and to make Laws. The interesting thing is that in a democracy, which is the historical basis for the use of the word 'Ekklesia', the Legislative Branch of Government had significant constitutional powers and was co-equal with the Executive Branch. So, when the Lord stated His intention to build the Church, He went on to designate legislative authority when He declared, "Whatever you bind in the earth would have been bound in Heaven (the Executive Branch), and whatever you allow in the earth realm would have already been allowed in the heavens." The real idea here is that Heaven would back up the Legislative Branch and execute its decisions.

The Church, then, is God's Legislative Executive—Congress—in a manner of speaking. We need to capture this concept as we advance in our prayer life with God. Ours is the responsibility to legislate in the city and for the city. When the Lord said He was building His 'Ekklesia', we know that He was speaking of His spiritual kingdom. He was, in fact, laying the axe at the root of the world systems. The Church is called to function in the Spirit, and so control all earthly powers and administrative systems. The enemy has caused many in the Church to think of our spiritual privileges as somehow of less significance and of lesser influence. Nothing could be further from the truth. Watch the incredible expansion of the Kingdom upon the earth and see how it has already shaped human history, law, politics and Government in general.

We must now begin to pray with a new vocabulary. Ours is the responsibility to overthrow, decree, declare, prohibit, fund, heal, set boundaries and borders, allow and disallow. We are to control territories, cultures, wealth, values and convictions. The Church has to rise up to legislate against the devil and demonic spirits that rule over the darkest regions of our time and evict them, so that we can coronate Jesus our Lord, as King of Kings—the ultimate Ruler.

There are several layers of truth embedded in Matthew 16:17-19, that would serve us well to uncover. For the purpose of moving on to a dimension of prayer in which we issue commands and directives to the material world and to demon spirits, we must make the effort to dig out every piece of vital information from the Word of God that we can. We may not, at this point, begin to give patterns of prayer, which we will, but we are providing the intercessor with the intellectual and spiritual construct to empower and validate this dimension. I think this is of great importance. My spiritual father once sat in my office and spelled out "theological inaccuracies" in this doctrine. As we began to discuss, he simply and humbly yielded to it. It was then and there that I came to realize that we must fill our minds and heart with truth and not just casually play around with fanciful light talk, exciting people with itching ears. So, let's begin to uncover layers of truth in this passage.

1. **The Church is to function as the Legislative Executive of the Kingdom of God.** This sudden interjection of the term 'Ekklesia' by the Lord, is deemed to be strategic. It was His intention to signal to His people and to principalities that they were on the verge of a radical takeover, and that a new political system had come upon the earth.

2. **The Kingdom of God is superior to, and is destined to, rule over all other kingdoms of the earth.** Because the Lord Jesus did not apply for consent from the earthly political systems, it is evident that He deemed His Authority to be at a higher level. Then, the fact that He stated that the gates of Hell (Hades) would not and cannot overcome His kingdom, it is obvious that God's Kingdom is superior in power, nature, and values. The kingdoms of this world *must* become the Kingdom of our God and of His Christ (Revelation 11:15).

3. **The Kingdom of God is carrying out a frontal assault upon the kingdom of Darkness.** As we, God's Legislative Executive, bow to pray, we are leveraging irresistible spiritual power against the enemy. This, my friend, is perpetual warfare until the Lord Jesus physically returns to the Planet.

4. **The Kingdom of God is revolutionary to all oppressive political systems.** It's war strategy is the complete overthrow of all secular systems. By 'secular', I refer to all operations upon the earth where the Bible is not acknowledged as the final rule of faith and doctrine, and Jesus is not acknowledged as Lord! Because these systems tend to be determined not to yield, the Kingdom of God adopts a revolutionary

strategy in the Spirit to dismantle these strongholds. It demands that eternal bondage of any people group is intolerable. It stands to enforce and maintain the achievements of Calvary. God's Kingdom supports the fact that no satanic system can hold back the liberation of God's people anywhere. The 'Ekklesia' is to create a revolution through its imposition of the values of God's Kingdom upon the earth through steadfast Governmental prayers.

5. **In Christ, the citizens of the Kingdom of God are trained for rulership,** and we signal that a new regime is upon the earth, destined to completely overthrow diabolical bureaucracies. It has been rightly stated that we are destined for the Throne, and that the earth's adversities are the context for our training for reigning. We are in a season of learning to wield the sword of the Spirit and to travail successfully in prayer. We are to learn the forces of royalty and government. We are the lawful heirs of Abraham and possessors of the earth, for the material world was given to righteous man. This facet must be embedded in our spirits and minds, so we can arise with wisdom and purpose and reconfigure our prayers.

6. **The citizens of the Kingdom of God are not just the recipients of justice, but also**

the agents chosen to administer justice upon the earth.

¹ Dare any of you, having a matter against another, go to law before the unjust, and not before the saints? **² Do ye not know that the saints shall judge the world?** *and if the world shall be judged by you, are ye unworthy to judge the smallest matters? ³ Know ye not that we shall judge angels? how much more things that pertain to this life?* (1 Corinthians 6:1-3 - KJV - Emphasis Added)

7. **One of the chief weapons of God's Kingdom is bold and authoritative prayer.** In this context, the Lord did not switch from asking the Church to pray. No, He told them "to bind and to loose." He told them "***whatever…***"; this speaks of the initiative of the Church on earth, executing its preferences and choices. Whatever you bind, or whatever you prevent is prevented; and whatever you loose, or allow, is allowed. These are not just moral sanctions; these are governmental issues, as we will see. You and I must take charge over the systems of earth and bring them into submission to the Lord and make them serve the purposes of God.

   The Church does not participate in bloody revolutions. We are a 'spiritual' kingdom. It is allowable and advised that we release Kingdom Activists into earthly systems, but our chief strategy is to rule in the Spirit. Because it sounds abstract, it is often thought of as trivial and powerless. However, this is far from the truth. Observe how the Lord operated. Through the Spirit, He changed nations and is still effecting change today. Look at how Daniel impacted history from the place of his spirit through prayer. Look how Joseph changed a nation's economy, first in the spiritual realm, then in the natural. Look how Elijah impacted the GDP of the nation from his knees. He knelt on the elements and so knelt on the economy.

8. **The Kingdom of God is expected to have complete economic autonomy, superseding the world's systems.** It does not exalt a vertical building of wealth, but a horizontal reciprocity of riches. Hence, 'giving' is pivotal to all its operations. It has always been the design of God that the Kingdom be a wealth-creating machine, and not just a group of individuals distributing and redistributing money.

9. **God's Kingdom is to be the most thriving sector of Economic Activity upon the earth.** Until all other Micro- or Macro- activities become impoverished, prayers should be configured by this reality. We are to call upon the wisdom of God to provoke entrepreneurship in the

Body of Christ. Prayer should produce witty inventions and fresh money-making ideas.

10. **The Kingdom of God does not support the elevation of one people group over the other.** It violently attempts to equalize all the peoples of the earth under the Lordship of Jesus, our Savior. Our prayers should always be configured by a stern demand upon world systems to bring an equalization of all the peoples of the earth. This equalization must be shaped by a mutual dependency on the gifts, talents, research, science and technology present in each other. Such is the nature of the Kingdom of God.

Considering these things, we must now shape a new vocabulary and develop fresh concepts for the prayers of the modern Church. The Church that Christ is building, prays from the above-mentioned perspective. Therefore, the following elements should be present in our prayers:

1. The word **'prayer'** must be understood, not only as making a request to God, but placing firm commands upon the material universe, the angelic hosts, Satan and his band of cohorts.

   ¹² Then Joshua spoke to the Lord on the day when the Lord gave the Amorites over to the Israelites, and he said in the sight of Israel, Sun, be silent and stand still at Gibeon, and you, moon, in the Valley of Ajalon! ¹³ And the sun stood still, and the moon stayed, until the nation took vengeance upon their enemies. Is not

this written in the Book of Jasher? So the sun stood still in the midst of the heavens and did not hasten to go down for about a whole day. ¹⁴ There was no day like it before or since, when the Lord heeded the voice of a man. For the Lord fought for Israel. (Joshua 10:12-14 - AMPC)

2. **Decrees:** A formal and authoritative order, especially one having the force of a law. It is also a statement describing the eternal purposes of God by which events are foreordained. (dictionary.com). An example of this is the twenty-third Psalm. Most people read this Psalm and fail to notice that David is not making a request. He is actually making a succession of decrees regarding his perpetual and abundant supply from the hand of God.

¹ The Lord is my shepherd, I shall not be in want. ²He makes me lie down in green pastures, he leads me beside quiet waters, ³ he restores my soul. He guides me in paths of righteousness for his name's sake. ⁴Even though I walk through the valley of the shadow of death, I will fear no evil, for you are with me; your rod and your staff, they comfort me. ⁵ You prepare a table before me in the presence of my enemies. You anoint my head with oil; my cup overflows. ⁶ Surely goodness and love will follow me all the days of my life, and I will dwell in the house of the Lord forever. (Psalm 23:1-6 - NIV)

3. **Declarations:** To make known or state clearly. The idea of a Declaration is to make plain or clear with a view to make payable—to make a dividend payable. When used in prayer, it carries the idea of calling upon that which is due by way of legal claim, contract, or covenant; establishing one's justifiable and legal claim to a thing. We, therefore, establish that which is now due through declarations.

4. **Charters:** We may not see this word in the Bible, but its concept is clearly stated. The online dictionary *(dictionary.com)* defines a 'charter' this way: it is a document that is issued by a sovereign nation outlining the conditions under which a colony, organization, or body is to operate. It defines rights, benefits, and privileges.

   Bearing this definition in mind, I think the concept of the will of God or the covenants of God documented in Scripture are to be considered as Charters. As we pray, it is vital that we rehearse the terms of the covenant and of the established will of God. Here is an example:

   [22] But you have come to Mount Zion, to the city of the living God, the heavenly Jerusalem. You have come to thousands upon thousands of angels in joyful assembly, [23] to the church of the firstborn, whose

names are written in heaven. You have come to God, the Judge of all, to the spirits of the righteous made perfect, ^{24} to Jesus the mediator of a new covenant, and to the sprinkled blood that speaks a better word than the blood of Abel. ^{25} See to it that you do not refuse him who speaks. If they did not escape when they refused him who warned them on earth, how much less will we, if we turn away from him who warns us from heaven? ^{26} At that time his voice shook the earth, but now he has promised, "Once more I will shake not only the earth but also the heavens." ^{27}The words "once more" indicate the removing of what can be shaken—that is, created things—so that what cannot be shaken may remain. ^{28} Therefore, **since we are receiving a kingdom that cannot be shaken**, *let us be thankful, and so worship God acceptably with reverence and awe, ^{29} for our "God is a consuming fire."* (Hebrews 12:22-29 - NIV - Emphasis Added)

And again, this passage defines the active and legal rights of benefits, access and operations:

^{15} [Christ, the Messiah] is therefore the Negotiator and Mediator of an [entirely] new agreement (testament, covenant), so that those who are called and offered it may receive the fulfillment of the promised everlasting inheritance – since a death has taken place which rescues and delivers and redeems them from the transgressions committed under the [old] first agreement. ^{16} For where there is a [last] will and

testament involved, the death of the one who made it must be established, ¹⁷ For a will and testament is valid and takes effect only at death, since it has no force or legal power as long as the one who made it is alive. ¹⁸ So even the [old] first covenant (God's will) was not inaugurated and ratified and put in force without the shedding of blood. ¹⁹ For when every command of the Law had been read out by Moses to all the people, he took the blood of slain calves and goats, together with water and scarlet wool and with a bunch of hyssop, and sprinkled both the Book (the roll of the Law and covenant) itself and all the people, ²⁰ Saying these words: This is the blood that seals and ratifies the agreement (the testament, the covenant) which God commanded [me to deliver to] you. (Hebrews 9:15-20 - AMPC)

When we enter the place of strategic prayers, we should rehearse the charter which we have, legitimizing our authority and right of function in the earth.

Here is a demonstration: *"This day I stand before the Sovereign Ruler of the Universe. I raise to His remembrance and notice that Christ the Messiah mediated and negotiated this charter on my behalf. Through His death on the Cross, He has provided me legitimate access to the Kingdom of God, the throne of Heaven, and abundant access to all the resources of Heaven. I establish as a legal recipient of salvation that all my sins are wiped away and all pain and* *suffering completed in Christ. Hence, I am not condemned, nor am I living in fear of divine judgement. Since Christ is risen and sits at the right hand of God, His last will and testament is now valid, enforced, and is in force. Hence, I have the life of God and walk in the nature of God. Now I am the Righteousness of God and the rightful heir of the world. I am a master of the material world and a master of demons and devils."*

5. **Prohibitions:** This word may have shades of meaning, but for the purpose of this discussion, I use the term 'prohibition' to mean defining boundaries for enemy combatants, foreign entities, movements of the elements and the such like. Prohibitions are designed to stop mutation and spread of virus germs and bacteria. It sets up boundaries around institutions, families and individuals. We may consider Psalm 91 as an example of a 'statement of prohibition' that is worthwhile for us to lift up in prayer often.

[1] Whoever dwells in the shelter of the Most High will rest in the shadow of the Almighty. [2] I will say of the Lord, "He is my refuge and my fortress, my God, in whom I trust." [3] Surely he will save you from the fowler's snare and from the deadly pestilence. [4] He will cover you with his feathers, and under his wings you will find refuge; his faithfulness will be

your shield and rampart. ⁵ You will not fear the terror of night, nor the arrow that flies by day, ⁶ nor the pestilence that stalks in the darkness, nor the plague that destroys at midday. ⁷ A thousand may fall at your side, ten thousand at your right hand, but it will not come near you. ⁸ You will only observe with your eyes and see the punishment of the wicked. ⁹ If you say, "The Lord is my refuge," and you make the Most High your dwelling, ¹⁰ no harm will overtake you, no disaster will come near your tent. ¹¹ For he will command his angels concerning you to guard you in all your ways; ¹² they will lift you up in their hands, so that you will not strike your foot against a stone. ¹³You will tread upon the lion and the cobra; you will trample the great lion and the serpent. (Psalm 91:1-13 - NIV)

6. **Appropriations:** The *Merriam Webster Online Dictionary* defines an 'appropriation' as, 'to take exclusive possession of, or to set apart for, or assign to a particular purpose'. It is a formal insistence of setting money or resources apart for a designated use. Such is the function of the U.S. Congress. They would appropriate money and resources for the nation's budget, for example, the building of the President's Border Wall.

   This is true in a biblical way as well. We see men of God who understood this dimension accomplish great things regarding the economies of nations. Elijah caused a recession and reduced the GDP of Israel, and then reversed it with prayer.

17 Elijah was a human being with a nature such as we have [with feelings, affections, and a constitution like ours]; and **he prayed earnestly for it not to rain, and no rain fell on the earth** *for three years and six months.* [1 Kings 17:1.] *18 And [then] he prayed again and the heavens supplied rain and the land produced its crops [as usual].* [1 Kings 18:42-45.] (James 5:17-18 - AMPC - Emphasis Added)

Another scriptural example of 'Appropriations' can be found in Isaiah 60:4-9:

4 "Lift up your eyes and look about you: All assemble and come to you; your sons come from afar, and your daughters are carried on the hip. 5 Then you will look and be radiant, your heart will throb and swell with joy; the wealth on the seas will be brought to you, to you the riches of the nations will come. 6 Herds of camels will cover your land, young camels of Midian and Ephah. And all from Sheba will come, bearing gold and incense and proclaiming the praise of the Lord. 7 All Kedar's flocks will be gathered to you, the rams of Nebaioth will serve you; they will be accepted as offerings on my altar, and I will adorn my glorious temple. 8 "Who are these that fly along like clouds, like doves to their nests? 9 Surely the islands look to me; in the lead are the ships of Tarshish, bringing your children from afar, with their silver and gold, to the honor of the Lord your God, the Holy One of Israel, for he has endowed you with splendor. (Isaiah 60:4-9 - NIV)

We should incorporate these verses of scripture in our prayer and formulate decrees and declarations for the appropriation of resources for our families, for our churches, institutions, and nations.

⁶ [Remember] this: he who sows sparingly and grudgingly will also reap sparingly and grudgingly, and he who sows generously [that blessings may come to someone] will also reap generously and with blessings. ⁷ Let each one [give] as he has made up his own mind and purposed in his heart, not reluctantly or sorrowfully or under compulsion, for God loves (He takes pleasure in, prizes above other things, and is unwilling to abandon or to do without) a cheerful (joyous, "prompt to do it") giver [whose heart is in his giving]. [Proverbs 22:9]. ⁸ And God is able to make all grace (every favor and earthly blessing) come to you in abundance, so that you may always and under all circumstances and whatever the need be self-sufficient [possessing enough to require no aid or support and furnished in abundance for every good work and charitable donation]. (2 Corinthians 9:6-8 - AMPC)

Do you observe the act of appropriation here? *"I declare upon you that you shall have all earthly blessings and every needed favor. You shall have enough in all circumstances. I decree that you shall have enough so that you will not need any human support and become completely materially self-sufficient."*

7. **Commands:** From a biblical perspective, a command is an order by God from which there is no retreat, and about which there is no choice but to obey. We were made in the image and likeness of God, and so we are *like* God, and we *represent* God. In this regard, as God's representatives in the earth, we are also expected to issue commands over the Kingdom of Satan and over the material universe.

   Through the issuance of commands, we—the blood-washed saints—are qualified to *order* the movements of demons; to *command* the enemy. We were told by our Lord to *drive out* demons; not *ask* them to leave. **Cast them out!**

   [17] And these signs will accompany those who believe: **In my name,** *they will* **drive out demons**; (Mark 16:17 - NIV - Emphasis Added)

   Through the discharging of commands, we are to bind them or prohibit them. We are credentialed by Heaven to set boundaries for the enemy and tell him how far to go.

   When you forcefully command the enemy as you stand in your redemptive place, you are issuing directives to him. As far as you are concerned, he has no choice but to obey, and he cannot retreat. He has to **immediately** obey.

When the Lord sent out His disciples to preach, they came back rejoicing because the devils were subject to them. Here is what the Lord said about what was happening in the world of the Spirit.

18 He replied, "I saw Satan fall like lightning from heaven. 19 I have given you authority to trample on snakes and scorpions and to overcome all the power of the enemy; nothing will harm you. (Luke 10:18-19 - NIV)

There are a few pertinent facts that we can glean from this text:

1) **Satan fell.** Note here that Satan had already been banished from the Heaven of heavens, so this may not have been what the Lord was referring to. 'Satan falling', I am convinced, was as a result of the spiritual operations of the apostles. 'Falling' carries the idea of him losing control. When a person falls, it is because they have lost balance, a foothold, or strength to stand. When the apostles dealt with him as they preached the Word, he lost control over the region and territory.

2) **Satan fell like Lightning.** Note that it is not only that he fell or lost control over the region, but he fell like lightning or at

lightning speed; his falling was immediate. Satan released control and was displaced with immediate timing or without delay. Often, we think that it takes hours or years for the enemy to be dislodged and dislocated. At the commands of the Apostles, he was instantly removed.

3) **Jesus gave us AUTHORITY to trample on snakes and scorpions and over ALL the power of the enemy.** The authority to command, stretches into the dimension of the satanic realm and enables us to shatter the enemy's power in strategic ways. When Jesus used words such as 'snakes' and 'scorpions', He was revealing crucial information about how the satanic kingdom operates. The Greek word for 'snake' used here is *'ophis'* [pronounced o-fes]; it refers to the malicious intentions of the enemy and how he gathers intelligence on you to gradually dismantle the assets in your life. It is the sly and cunning activity of the enemy.

The other word used here is 'scorpion'. The Greek word *'skorpios'* [pronounced skor-pe'-os] means 'to conceal oneself with deadly intentions'. The idea here is of an 'ambushment'. The enemy secretly plots your demise and attempts to destroy you with a sudden, unexpected attack. His ancient strategy is to use unexpected people at unexpected times. He has mastered the art of surprise. However, when diabolical strategies are prophetically revealed, and commands given by God's Legislative Executive, and confinements decided, Satan **has to** obey! Our commands issue a 'restraining order'; a 'cease and desist'; a 'search and destroy' decree, which every enemy combatant **must** submit to without delay.

8. **Proclamations:** Most online dictionaries define a 'proclamation' as 'an official announcement, or official document announcing something of importance'. The announcement is often used to give value to a people or organization. It is used as in the case of a President declaring a state of affairs, as in a federal emergency. This announcement provides the context of public recognition and participation with.

⁷ I will proclaim the Lord's decree: He said to me, "You are my Son; today I have become your Father. ⁸Ask me, and I will make the nations your inheritance, the ends of the earth your possession. ⁹ You will break them with a rod of iron; you will dash them to pieces like pottery." ¹⁰ Therefore, you kings, be wise; be warned, you rulers of the earth. ¹¹ Serve the Lord with fear and celebrate his rule with trembling. (Psalm 2:7-11 - NIV)

¹¹ The Lord has made proclamation to the ends of the earth: "Say to the Daughter of Zion, 'See, your Savior comes! See, his reward is with him, and his recompense accompanies him.'" ¹² They will be called the Holy People, the Redeemed of the Lord; and you will be called Sought After, the City No Longer Deserted. (Isaiah 62:11-12 - NIV)

9. **Creeds:** The Merriam Online Dictionary defines a 'creed' as 'a set of fundamental beliefs'. The word is derived from the Latin word 'Credo' meaning: 'I Believe'. Creeds shape the paradigm, or the set of dispositions, behind choices and actions. They propel and activate behavior.

When we pray, there is a place for the establishment of creeds. When we speak them authoritatively, we are developing strongholds for accurate behavior. Many of us have come to know that 'right thinking' produces 'right behavior'. We change behavior by the transformation of the mind. There must be a shift in the paradigm. The authoritative speaking of creeds has the potential to break bad habits and establish new strongholds; righteous strongholds in our lives.

In our next chapter, we will formulate patterns of creeds as a guide for us to follow.

We must accept that the Kingdom of God somewhat resembles a totalitarian or dictatorial Governmental System, but without the oppression usually attached to these forms of rulership. God has raised us up as a 'Congress' upon the earth to participate with Him in the governance of human society, the control of demons, and the management of the material universe. The Lord's statement that we have been given permission to "Bind and Loose", are not just casual words. The essence of what He was saying is that whatever the Legislative Branch of the Government decides on earth, then Heaven—the Executive Branch—will execute it.

Prayer

Dear Master, I take my place as a member of your legislative executive. I agree to legislate appropriations for the Kingdom of God and for hurting humanity. Today I agree to take my place in the 'Supreme Court of the Universe', as a member of the 'Global Tribunal', and execute the judgements written against rebellious nations and satanic agents. You have raised me up and caused me to sit with Christ in the heavenly realms to reign and rule with Him. Grant me the grace and the discipline to execute these most serious duties with skillfulness of hand and integrity of heart, in Jesus' name, Amen.

WE ARE GOD'S LEGISLATIVE EXECUTIVE

NOTES

"MAN HAS BEEN DESIGNATED THE RULER, THE MANAGER, THE MARSHAL OF THE MATERIAL UNIVERSE, WITH LIMITLESS POSSIBILITIES."

CHAPTER 8

Rulers of the Material World

As we advance into this new way of praying, we must add to our inner convictions, this awareness that God made man to be the ruler over the material world. This is really the original design and purpose for the creation of man. Therefore, we are to pray as if we are already in possession of the things we need. We are to speak authoritatively as though a ruler over things.

It is important to note that in the book of Genesis, the first commandment given to man was not to attend church anywhere. It was not to love your neighbor as yourself. It was not even to love the Lord your God. The first commandment given to man was not to be a worshipper. Some may say that it was His intention that we be sabbath keepers. None of those positions took center-stage at the inception. The first command given to man was to **"Be fruitful."**

> ²⁸ *God blessed them and said to them,* **"Be fruitful** *and increase in number; fill the earth and subdue it. Rule over the fish in the sea and the birds in the sky and over every living creature that moves on the ground."* (Genesis 1:28 - NIV - Emphasis Added)

This is very interesting, because it creates a new paradigm and spiritual platform in which we are called to pray.

To be 'fruitful' is to be 'productive'. His was the requirement to use the raw materials of the Garden and develop goods and services for his comfort and that of his family. God knew that the earth contained a limitless volume of possibilities and challenged man to begin the process of creative thinking and creative production. Note, as well, that the man was given the assignment to dress and to keep the Garden.

> ¹⁵ *And the Lord God took the man, and put him into the garden of Eden to dress it and to keep it.* (Genesis 2:15 - KJV)

This endorses the point that we are making in this chapter. The Psalms further accentuate it:

> ⁴ *What is man that You are mindful of him, and the son of [earthborn] man that You care for him?* ⁵ *Yet You have made him but a little lower than God [or heavenly beings], and You have crowned him with glory and honor.* ⁶ *You made him to have dominion over the works of Your hands; You have put all things under his feet:* ⁷ *All sheep and oxen, yes, and the beasts of the field,* ⁸ *The birds of the air, and the fish of the sea, and whatever passes along the paths of*

the seas. ⁹ O Lord, our Lord, how excellent (majestic and glorious) is Your name in all the earth! (Psalm 8:4-9 - AMPC)

Firstly, man was made with the rank, "a little lower than God." He out-ranks angels, demons and all created things. Secondly, **God** crowned him. This means that his presence is the presence of royalty and majesty. His presence is the imitation of God. The way he is seen by the rest of creation is as if God is present. This is what it means to be in the likeness and the image of God. This passage teaches that God made man to rule over every other created thing. Thirdly, we may logically deduce that the spiritual, mental and physical design of the man was to equip him with the abilities of a ruler. God made, God designed man. God wired him with the divine circuitry to be a ruler. Equally, He designed creation to respond to the man. All creatures are made to submit to the 'image of God' upon the earth.

The Message version of the Bible does a great job on this passage and offers a stunning revelation.

> *³ I look up at your macro-skies, dark and enormous, your handmade sky-jewelry, Moon and stars mounted in their settings. ⁴ Then I look at my micro-self and wonder, why do you bother with us? Why take a second look our way? ⁵ Yet we've so narrowly missed being gods, bright with Eden's dawn light. ⁶ You put us in charge of your handcrafted world, repeated to us your Genesis-charge, ⁷ Made us lords of sheep and cattle, even animals out in the wild, ⁸ Birds flying and fish*

swimming, whales singing in the ocean deeps. (Psalm 8:3-8 - MSG)

This is an uncommon perspective.

1. The Psalmist looks into the massiveness of the Universe, not only to marvel at it—though it is quite marvelous—but to elaborate on the power of God in man and to stand in awe of God's mindfulness of us.

2. He takes a look, not just at how small a man is in structure, but even though man is intricately woven with microscopic particles that are infinitely smaller than the vastness of the material world, our majestic God still takes the time to consider us. The implication of this statement is what stimulates the thought that God Himself is amazed at His own handiwork in man. For it is in God's consideration of the incredible power of the micro-man that directed David to perceive that we just nearly missed being God Himself. It is in this realm of subatomic particles that man is clearly wired to manage the world that is so vast and magnificent.

3. The Psalmist also establishes that there is a legal tender in who has managerial rights to the world. God says He made us—His people—to have dominion, or to be ruler over the material world. The Hebrew word

for 'ruler' in this passage is 'MASHAL'...very similar to the English word 'Marshal'. The man is the 'Marshal' of the Universe. His is the responsibility to ensure that the Universe behaves the way God designed it, and to use his superior mental powers to maintain the use of its resources for his comfort.

4. The man was to tame the wild animals and not fear them. He was to fly higher than birds and move faster than animals. He was to swim longer and deeper that the fish of the sea. According to these verses they all exist for the comfort of man.

Apart from creative activity, man was designed the alter the course of nature and to subdue any performance of nature that acted hostile to the purposes of God and the tranquility of man. It was God who intended that through the spoken word, and through the power of prayer, the world would submit to him. Here is a mountain of evidence:

1. Noah Spoke to The Animals

17 I am going to bring floodwaters on the earth to destroy all life under the heavens, every creature that has the breath of life in it. Everything on earth will perish. 18 But I will establish my covenant with you, and you will enter the ark – you and your sons and your wife and your sons' wives with you. 19 You are to bring into the ark two of all living creatures, male

> *and female, to keep them alive with you. ²⁰ Two of every kind of bird, of every kind of animal and of every kind of creature that moves along the ground will come to you to be kept alive. ²¹ You are to take every kind of food that is to be eaten and store it away as food for you and for them." ²² Noah did everything just as God commanded him.* (Genesis 6:17-22 - NIV)

Note here that Noah obeyed God and took a pair of every animal that God had made into the ark to preserve its life. Several important points are to be considered. Firstly, he had to possess accurate knowledge of every creature God created. Secondly, Noah had to know how to identify the male and the female. Thirdly, he had to know which ones were dangerous and tame them.

> *²⁵ God made the wild animals according to their kinds...* (Genesis 1:25a - NIV)

Finally, Noah had to possess some way to get them into the ark in an orderly and efficient manner. It had to be that Noah and his children had ways of speaking to the animal kingdom in a manner that they understood; even the birds which would be high in the sky. It must have been normal for them to call birds from a distance. All of these logical conclusions fit the revelation that the man was the 'Marshal', the 'ruler' of the material world.

> *¹³ On that very day Noah and his sons, Shem, Ham and Japheth, together with his wife and the wives of his three sons, entered the ark. ¹⁴ They had with them*

every wild animal according to its kind, all livestock according to their kinds, every creature that moves along the ground according to its kind and every bird according to its kind, everything with wings. ¹⁵ *Pairs of all creatures that have the breath of life in them came to Noah and entered the ark.* ¹⁶ *The animals going in were male and female of every living thing, as God had commanded Noah. Then the Lord shut him in.* (Genesis 7:13-16 - NIV)

2. Joshua Commanded the Sun

¹² *On the day the Lord gave the Amorites over to Israel, Joshua said to the Lord in the presence of Israel: "Sun, stand still over Gibeon, and you, moon, over the Valley of Aijalon."* ¹³ *So the sun stood still, and the moon stopped, till the nation avenged itself on its enemies, as it is written in the Book of Jashar. The sun stopped in the middle of the sky and delayed going down about a full day.* ¹⁴ *There has never been a day like it before or since, a day when the Lord listened to a human being. Surely the Lord was fighting for Israel!* (Joshua 10:12-14 - NIV)

This is most incredible. The miracle that happened here is stunning and amazing. Here are some issues in this manifestation.

a) This miracle was initiated by Joshua. A **man** had taken command over the material world to have it respond to his assignment.

b) He had no promise from God upon which to base his faith for that particular feat.

c) When Joshua spoke to the sun, he was talking to the Lord. He said to the Lord, "Sun, stand still." It is interesting that the Word says, "God listened to a man." What this means is that when Joshua was speaking to the sun, God listened to him and worked to make what his servant said come to pass.

d) Not only did he tell the sun and the moon to stop moving, but he told them *where* to stop.

e) The sun stopped for a full day. This means that when Joshua spoke, the entire material world stopped its aging process, and the entire galaxy stopped.

f) This proves that the micro-man has been deputized by Heaven to control the macro-world. The sun has a radius of 432,169 miles and a diameter of 865,000 miles. The earth's diameter is only 7,917.5 miles in comparison. Think of the magnitude of the sun over the earth. The sun is 109 times bigger than the earth. Then think about the miniature size of Joshua standing on the earth decreeing a 'stand still' to these massive structures, and the sun and the moon obeyed him for an entire day—a mind-blowing reality.

g) The Hebrew expression "so the sun stood still," implies that it hurried to stop, or that the action of the sun in responding to the words of the servant of God was as if it came to a screeching halt. It hurried to stand still.

3. Jesus Spoke to the Wind and Waves

³⁹ And he arose, and rebuked the wind, and said unto the sea, Peace, be still. And the wind ceased, and there was a great calm. ⁴⁰ And he said unto them, Why are ye so fearful? how is it that ye have no faith? (Mark 4:39-40 - KJV)

In this instance, we see the Lord talking to the weather. He rebuked the wind and He spoke peace to the warring elements of the waves. Then He told off the disciples, upbraiding them for their unbelief. It is easy to see, then, that the entire world was designed to respond to the righteous. Our Lord spoke as if annoyed that the disciples woke Him instead of performing the required miracle themselves with the same authority.

4. Jesus Spoke to A Tree

¹³ Seeing in the distance a fig tree in leaf, he went to find out if it had any fruit. When he reached it, he found nothing but leaves, because it was not the season for figs. ¹⁴ Then he said to the tree, "May no one ever eat fruit from you again." And his disciples heard him say it. (Mark 11:13-14 - NIV)

On the surface, Christ's angry response to a non-bearing tree makes Him appear very irrational. The tree not bearing fruit was no fault of its own. It was not its season to bear fruit. You would have thought that the Lord would have known that. Additionally, the curse was a permanent thing. He told it that from that moment forward, it would not bear fruit. In approximately twenty-four hours the fig tree dried up from the roots, according to verse 20.

> [20] *In the morning, as they went along, they saw the fig tree withered from the roots.* [21] *Peter remembered and said to Jesus, "Rabbi, look! The fig tree you cursed has withered!"* (Mark 11:20-21 - NIV)

An astonished group of disciples saw the impact of their Lord's words as they passed by the cursed tree a second time and observed its withered condition. What, at first, could have been interpreted as irrational behavior on Jesus' part, was actually the Lord teaching His disciples a tremendous lesson in faith.

> [22] *"Have faith in God," Jesus answered.* [23] *"Truly I tell you, if anyone says to this mountain, 'Go, throw yourself into the sea,' and does not doubt in his heart but believes that what they say will happen, it will be done for them.* [24] *Therefore I tell you, whatever you ask for in prayer, believe that you have received it, and it will be yours.* [25] *And when you stand praying, if you hold anything against anyone, forgive them, so that your Father in heaven may forgive you your sins."* (Mark 11:22-25 - NIV)

The lesson learnt here is that the material world responds to faith-filled words. The Lord expanded their possibilities in a greater way by letting them know the magnitude of what they could achieve. He told them they could talk to a mountain and the mountain would respond. He even informed them that they would be able to do greater works than what they had seen Him do.

> [12] *Very truly I tell you, whoever believes in me will do the* **works** *I have been doing, and they will do even* **greater** *things than these...* (John 14:12a - NIV)

Let me emphasize this point: Man has been designated the ruler, the manager, the marshal of the material universe, with limitless possibilities.

5. He Turned Water into Wine

> [7] *Jesus said to the servants, "Fill the jars with water"; so they filled them to the brim.* [8] *Then he told them, "Now draw some out and take it to the master of the banquet." They did so,* [9] *and the master of the banquet tasted the water that had been turned into wine. He did not realize where it had come from, though the servants who had drawn the water knew. Then he called the bridegroom aside* [10] *and said, "Everyone brings out the choice wine first and then the cheaper wine after the guests have had too much to drink; but you have saved the best till now."* (John 2:7-10 - NIV)

Without doing a complete exposition on this passage, it is important to see that the Lord turned water—plain, natural water—into wine. It is commonly believed that it takes about ten to fifteen days to make wine. Some say you need to leave it for about four to twelve months. If this is true, and it does seem this way, the Lord's words over the wine accelerated the fermentation process of the water in just a matter of minutes. Though the Bible is silent on the kind of wine, it must have had good taste, since the people thought it was the 'best'. So, the Lord injected, with His blessing on it, some additive for taste. Again, this establishes that man is the master of the material world and has the right to alter it.

6. Transcend the Law of Time, Effort, Motion

21 Then they were willing to take him into the boat, and immediately the boat reached the shore where they were heading. (John 6:21 - NIV)

Here we see that the Lord entered a ship with the disciples, and without any delay, the boat got to its destination. It arrived without journeying. In the words of the proverbial saying, "This is crazy!" Scientifically, this is what we call a 'quantum leap'.

The Message version of the Bible puts it better.

21 So they took him on board. In no time they reached land—the exact spot they were headed to. In no time they arrived at their destination. (John 6:21 - MSG)

'Quanta' is the smallest measurement of energy. It is that wave or particle that cannot be broken down any smaller. So, in an indivisible moment, they arrived. Again, the quantum leap is arrival without journeying. We see that it was as long as they were willing to let the Lord in on their ship that this miracle manifested.

The *Amplified Bible, Classic Edition* adds more clarity to the picture.

> *²¹ Then they were quite willing and glad for Him to come into the boat. And now the boat went at once to the land they had steered toward. [And immediately they reached the shore toward which they had been slowly making their way.]* (John 6:21 - AMPC)

Several beautiful principles are taught here. Our willingness to let the Lord into our 'ships', *per se*, is demonstrated by the joy brought about by walking with Him. For a quantum leap to take place, there must be heat. Heat excites the subatomic particles and causes them to leap out of orbit. 'Joy' is 'heat' in the spirit realm. It is being passionate or having a burning desire. Letting Christ into your 'ship' is not a passive thing. Instead, it is purposeful. 'Him on the ship', is Him participating and partnering with you in your business enterprises and your sense of direction in life.

Then we see that the direction they were heading in, and the place to which they were going, were supernaturally impacted on. He does not alter your personal goals to make them His; He wants to make your dreams come through as well. They got to the place to which they were steering. Finally, we see the issue of speed. The speed at which they were journeying was completely taken over and they enjoyed a quantum leap to their destination.

7. Multiplied Bread and Fish

⁴ The Jewish Passover Festival was near. ⁵ When Jesus looked up and saw a great crowd coming toward him, he said to Philip, "Where shall we buy bread for these people to eat?" ⁶ He asked this only to test him, for he already had in mind what he was going to do. ⁷Philip answered him, "It would take more than half a year's wages to buy enough bread for each one to have a bite!" ⁸ Another of his disciples, Andrew, Simon Peter's brother, spoke up, ⁹ "Here is a boy with five small barley loaves and two small fish, but how far will they go among so many?" ¹⁰ Jesus said, "Have the people sit down." There was plenty of grass in that place, and the men sat down (about five thousand men were there). ¹¹ Jesus then took the loaves, gave thanks, and distributed to those who were seated as much as they wanted. He did the same with the fish. ¹² When they had all had enough to eat, he said to his disciples, "Gather the pieces that are left over. Let nothing be wasted." ¹³ So they gathered them and filled twelve baskets with the pieces of the five barley loaves left over by those who had eaten. (John 6:4-13 - NIV)

This thousand-fold miracle is one of the most popular in the Bible. Our Lord took five loaves and a few fish and fed five thousand. The fact that they took up twelve baskets afterwards, seems to suggest something significant. The time of the event is the time of the Passover. This indicates that God wants us to enter into a new dimension of His workings in the earth.

The Passover celebrates the passing over of Israel from the bondage and slavery of Egypt to enter their promised land, the land that flows with milk and honey; the land of luxury and blessing. This miracle shows us how the Lord tapped into unseen resources. He did not command the bread or the fish to multiply; He did not ask the Father to multiply them. He merely gave thanks. To 'thank' is to 'take note of'. So, He took note of the things that were His, even if they were invisible. To pick up twelve baskets is also significant, because it refers to the feeding of the entire nation of Israel, God's people by extension. Hence, Christ was establishing that all of God's people have unhindered access to the same resources that He accessed that day.

8. He Healed Sick Bodies

Over and over throughout the ministry of the Lord Jesus, He healed the sick. In these various cases, He simply altered the state of the body. Here is a look at some of them:

a) He Heals an Official's Son in Capernaum

^{47} When this man heard that Jesus had arrived in Galilee from Judea, he went to him and begged him to come and heal his son, who was close to death. ^{48} "Unless you people see miraculous signs and wonders,"

Jesus told him, "you will never believe." ⁴⁹ The royal official said, "Sir, come down before my child dies." ⁵⁰ "Go," Jesus replied, "your son will live." (John 4:47-50 - NIV)

b) **Jesus Healed Peter's Mother-In-Law Who Had A Debilitating Fever**

¹⁴ When Jesus came into Peter's house, he saw Peter's mother-in-law lying in bed with a fever. ¹⁵ He touched her hand and the fever left her, and she got up and began to wait on him. (Matthew 8:14-15 - NIV)

c) **He Healed A Man Who Had Leprosy**

¹ When Jesus came down from the mountainside, large crowds followed him. ² A man with leprosy came and knelt before him and said, "Lord, if you are willing, you can make me clean." ³ Jesus reached out his hand and touched the man. "I am willing," he said. "Be clean!" Immediately he was cleansed of his leprosy. (Matthew 8:1-3 - NIV)

d) **He Healed A Woman Who Had A Running Blood Issue**

²⁵ And a woman was there who had been subject to bleeding for twelve years. ²⁶ She had suffered a great deal under the care of many doctors and had spent all she had, yet instead of getting better she grew worse. ²⁷When she heard about Jesus, she came up behind him in the crowd and touched his cloak, ²⁸ because she thought, "If I just touch his clothes, I will be

healed." ²⁹ Immediately her bleeding stopped and she felt in her body that she was freed from her suffering. ³⁰ At once Jesus realized that power had gone out from him. He turned around in the crowd and asked, "Who touched my clothes?" ³¹ "You see the people crowding against you," his disciples answered, "and yet you can ask, 'Who touched me?'" ³² But Jesus kept looking around to see who had done it. ³³ Then the woman, knowing what had happened to her, came and fell at his feet and, trembling with fear, told him the whole truth. ³⁴ He said to her, "Daughter, your faith has healed you. Go in peace and be freed from your suffering." (Mark 5:25-34 - NIV)

e) **He Brought A Dead Body Back to Life**

³⁷ He did not let anyone follow him except Peter, James and John the brother of James. ³⁸ When they came to the home of the synagogue ruler, Jesus saw a commotion, with people crying and wailing loudly. ³⁹ He went in and said to them, "Why all this commotion and wailing? The child is not dead but asleep." ⁴⁰ But they laughed at him. After he put them all out, he took the child's father and mother and the disciples who were with him, and went in where the child was. ⁴¹ He took her by the hand and said to her, "Talitha koum!" (which means, "Little girl, I say to you, get up!"). ⁴² Immediately the girl stood up and walked around (she was twelve years old). At this they were completely astonished. (Mark 5:37-42 - NIV)

f) Jesus Healed Two Blind Men

²⁷ As Jesus went on from there, two blind men followed him, calling out, "Have mercy on us, Son of David!" ²⁸ When he had gone indoors, the blind men came to him, and he asked them, "Do you believe that I am able to do this?" "Yes, Lord," they replied. ²⁹ Then he touched their eyes and said, "According to your faith let it be done to you"; ³⁰ and their sight was restored... (Matthew 9:27-30a - NIV)

g) He Heals A Man Who Could Not Speak

³² While they were going out, a man who was demon-possessed and could not talk was brought to Jesus. ³³ And when the demon was driven out, the man who had been mute spoke. The crowd was amazed and said, "Nothing like this has ever been seen in Israel." (Matthew 9:32-33 - NIV)

h) Jesus Heals an Invalid

⁴ Here a great number of disabled people used to lie— the blind, the lame, the paralyzed. ⁵ One who was there had been an invalid for thirty-eight years. ⁶When Jesus saw him lying there and learned that he had been in this condition for a long time, he asked him, "Do you want to get well?" ⁷ "Sir," the invalid replied, "I have no one to help me into the pool when the water is stirred. While I am trying to get in, someone else goes down ahead of me." ⁸ Then Jesus said to him, "Get up! Pick up your mat and walk." ⁹ At once the man was cured; he picked up his mat and walked. (John 5:3-9 - NIV)

i) **He Heals A Man by Using Spit**

⁶ After saying this, he spit on the ground, made some mud with the saliva, and put it on the man's eyes. ⁷ "Go," he told him, "wash in the Pool of Siloam" (this word means Sent). So the man went and washed, and came home seeing. (John 9:6-7 - NIV)

j) **He Heals A Man with A Sleep Disorder**

¹ It happened that when He went into the house of one of the leaders of the Pharisees on the Sabbath to eat bread, they were watching Him closely. ² And there in front of Him was a man suffering from dropsy. ³ And Jesus answered and spoke to the lawyers and Pharisees, saying, "Is it lawful to heal on the Sabbath, or not?" ⁴ But they kept silent. And He took hold of him and healed him, and sent him away. (Luke 14:1-4 - NASB)

k) **He Cleansed Ten Lepers**

¹¹ Now on his way to Jerusalem, Jesus traveled along the border between Samaria and Galilee. ¹² As he was going into a village, ten men who had leprosy met him. They stood at a distance ¹³ and called out in a loud voice, "Jesus, Master, have pity on us!" ¹⁴ When he saw them, he said, "Go, show yourselves to the priests." And as they went, they were cleansed. (Luke 17:11-14 - NIV)

l) **He Raised Lazarus From the Dead**

⁴³ When he had said this, Jesus called in a loud voice, "Lazarus, come out!" ⁴⁴ The dead man came out, his hands and feet wrapped with strips of linen, and a cloth around his face. (John 11:43-44 - NIV)

m) **He Restores Sight to Blind Bartimaeus**

⁴⁹ Jesus stopped and said, "Call him." So they called to the blind man, "Cheer up! On your feet! He's calling you." ⁵⁰ Throwing his cloak aside, he jumped to his feet and came to Jesus. ⁵¹ "What do you want me to do for you?" Jesus asked him. The blind man said, "Rabbi, I want to see." ⁵² "Go," said Jesus, "your faith has healed you." Immediately he received his sight and followed Jesus along the road. (Mark 10:49-52 - NIV)

In these miraculous cases, our Lord repaired organs and tissues. He chased out demons that caused ailments. In some cases, He repaired bodily functions such as seeing and hearing. He healed sleep disorders as well. These miracles clearly revealed Jesus' complete control and dominion over everything that is material—an ability which has also been graciously granted to us as sons of God, and God's executors in the earth.

9. Moses Parted the Red Sea with A Rod

¹³ Moses answered the people, "Do not be afraid. Stand firm and you will see the deliverance the Lord will bring you today. The Egyptians you see today you will never see again. ¹⁴ The Lord will fight for you; you need only to be still." ¹⁵ Then the Lord said to Moses, "Why are you crying out to me? Tell the Israelites to move on. ¹⁶ Raise your staff and stretch out your hand over the sea to divide the water so that the Israelites can go through the sea on dry ground. (Exodus 14:13-16 - NIV)

²¹ Then Moses stretched out his hand over the sea, and all that night the Lord drove the sea back with a strong east wind and turned it into dry land. The waters were divided, ²² and the Israelites went through the sea on dry ground, with a wall of water on their right and on their left. (Exodus 14:21-22 - NIV)

In my opinion, apart from the resurrection of Christ, this is by far the greatest, most spectacular miracle in the entire Bible. When Moses raised his rod at the command of the Lord, a wind blew a path in the sea and dried the floor. The waters stood up on the right and on the left and let the people of God through. A phenomenon of this magnitude happening, is utterly amazing. To think that God did this at the hand of Moses when he raised the rod, is corroborating evidence that we are masters of the material world.

10. The Priests Parted the Jordan With Their Feet

⁹ Joshua said to the Israelites, "Come here and listen to the words of the Lord your God. ¹⁰ This is how you will know that the living God is among you and that he will certainly drive out before you the Canaanites, Hittites, Hivites, Perizzites, Girgashites, Amorites and Jebusites. ¹¹ See, the ark of the covenant of the Lord of all the earth will go into the Jordan ahead of you. ¹² Now then, choose twelve men from the tribes of Israel, one from each tribe. ¹³ And as soon as the priests who carry the ark of the Lord—the Lord of all the earth—set foot in the Jordan, its waters flowing downstream will be cut off and stand up in a heap." (Joshua 3:9-13 - NIV)

I like the part when the Lord told them that, "This is how you will **know** that **the living God is among you…**" When we see the material world visibly complying to the commands and intentions of mortal man, we **know** that the living God is in the midst of His people.

11. Christ And Peter Walked on Water

²⁹ …Then Peter got down out of the boat, walked on the water and came toward Jesus. (Matthew 14:29 - NIV)

Peter did not walk on the water because of God's power, or he could not sink. It is not the will of God that kept him walking. If that were so, he could not sink because he was walking in obedience. The molecular structure of the water did not change so as to provide a firm footing for him. His walking on water had nothing to do with the presence of God. He was close to Jesus at the time. When he cried out for help, the Lord reached out a hand and caught him. His walking on the water had something to do with his mindset. It was when he finally saw the wind and the waves, and how threatening they were, another belief came to him. This is indeed a principle of stupendous proportion. Our thoughts and words manipulate the material world.

12. The Creation of Two Bears to Eat Forty-Two Children

²³ From there Elisha went up to Bethel. As he was walking along the road, some boys came out of the town and jeered at him. "Get out of here, baldy!" they said. "Get out of here, baldy!" ²⁴ He turned around, looked at them and called down a curse on them in the name of the Lord. Then two bears came out of the woods and mauled forty-two of the boys. (2 Kings 2:23-24 - NIV)

Another amazing case. Here we see that the man of God called down a curse upon the children and two bears came out of the woods and killed forty-two children. I am told that bears did not live in that area. If that is so, then his words created two animals. We also note that the animals did the bidding of the man of God, and they were not trained pets. These obedient bears did what the other animals did in the Noah episode, when they obeyed him and entered the ark.

13. Supernatural Transportation

³⁹ When they came up out of the water, the Spirit of the Lord suddenly took Philip away, and the eunuch did not see him again, but went on his way rejoicing. (Acts 8:39 - NIV)

²⁶ But Elisha said to him, "Was not my spirit with you when the man got down from his chariot to meet you? Is this the time to take money, or to accept clothes— or olive groves and vineyards, or flocks and herds, or male and female slaves? (2 Kings 5:26 - NIV)

In both of these cases, the two individuals were transported by the Spirit of God through time and space. It appears as if there is no limit to what can happen in the material world. Man's movement across the world is not bound by human modes of transportation.

The point that we have so adequately established is that man is the master of the material world and the material world is designed to respond to man's thoughts and his words. We observe that in the case of Christ, and He is the ministering example for us, He commanded the material world to conform to His preferences. The world is awaiting redeemed man who will take his rightful place, and function with 'Throne Room' authority.

Our decrees and declarations are meant to manage the world supernaturally. We are to establish our creeds, our systems of belief in various areas. We are to make proclamations and charters. When we speak, the elements in the environment work to transform themselves into the physical equivalent.

It might look a bit nutty to be talking to inanimate objects. Yet this was the practice of the Lord Jesus Christ. God wants us to stop worrying like peasants, and to think like royalty.

Kings do not ask for things. Kings live with the abiding recognition that all of their needs are met. We must be freed from the mentality of pauperhood. The world is our domain and our jurisdiction. We are to act like it is ours to manage, and so we must subdue it and have dominion over it.

We are to rule in the midst of the enemy. We must rule like kings. Part of the purpose of prayer is to mediate for the management of the material world.

Ask for Things

This current culture of Christianity makes praying for things somewhat a carnal and sinful habit. Even when there appears to be some kind of allowance for this type of request, many times the intentions of the heart of the seeker is viewed as suspicious. Christ, on the other hand, shows us that:

a) **We Need Things**

> [30] *If that is how God clothes the grass of the field, which is here today and tomorrow is thrown into the fire, will he not much more clothe you—you of little faith?* [31] *So do not worry, saying, 'What shall we eat?' or 'What shall we drink?' or 'What shall we wear?'* [32] *For the pagans run after all these things,* **and your heavenly Father knows that you need them**. (Matthew 6:30-32 - NIV - Emphasis Added)

b) **God Approves Our Desire for Things**

> [24] *Therefore I say unto you, What things soever ye desire, when ye pray, believe that ye receive them, and ye shall have them.* (Mark 11:24 - KJV)

The things of which Christ spoke in the Matthew passage have to do with food, clothing, and shelter. He points out that it is the Father's good pleasure to see His children with 'things'. We should never be ashamed of having a healthy ambition to acquire and consume personal possessions. God knows that you have need of them, and it is His delight to see you with them. It is for this reason that He gives us a body. Our anatomy and physiology establish this need. Our physical bodies have several needs, one of which is minerals in the food category. These minerals include Magnesium, Zinc, Iron, Calcium, Potassium and so on. Hence, anyone that attacks our need to possess things does not understand the order of God, nor the order of creation. God wants you to have things, and to have them in abundance.

We should boldly confess that our needs are met and that we are abundantly supplied. We are to forcefully make use of 'commands'—just as Jesus did with the wind and the waves. We should pray 'big' prayers in this 'Throne Room Dimension', knowing that God will give us exactly what we ask for in the material world.

Prayer

Great and Glorious God in Heaven, you have created me to be the master of the material world. You have intricately designed me with the mental and spiritual faculties to perform, with excellence, the responsibilities of management. Help me to be fruitful, to produce abundantly the fruit I create. Help me to leave a significant deposit behind for future generations, and to conquer the world through intelligent pursuit. Then help me to use the resources that we create together for the comforts of my family and the benefit of all around me. These things I ask in Jesus' name, Amen.

> "TAKE YOUR PLACE AROUND THE 'THRONE' AND PRAY LIKE A KING. PRAY LIKE YOU ARE AN AUTHENTIC CHILD OF GOD. PRAY WITH A NEW LEVEL OF CONFIDENCE."

CHAPTER 9

Intercessors In The Throne

As we advance into this new order of prayer, a revelation of the Throne of God is important. Though much is said about God's Throne, there is still much to learn, and as we develop our understanding, we are better able to pray with authority and confidence. The fact is, the plan of redemption redefines the nature of the believer to show that he is of 'divine stock'. It is clear that in redemption, God is divinizing man. He has the seed of God or the DNA of the Godhead. The fact that we are shown as being seated with Christ in Heavenly Places, indicate that the Body of Christ bears incredible authority in the administration of the Universe.

A Seat for Rulers to Sit In

Both the Hebrew word '*Kicce*', and the Greek word '*thronos*' translated 'throne,' refer to the same thing. They refer to the seat upon which the supreme leader of a kingdom or large organization sit for the formal execution of responsibilities or duties. Let us examine some important facts about the 'Throne of God'.

The Throne of God

a) **God Sits on A Throne Because He Is the Owner of The World and Is Its Sovereign Ruler.**

> *¹ In the year that King Uzziah died,* **I saw the Lord, high and exalted, seated on a throne**; *and the train of his robe filled the temple. ² Above him were seraphim, each with six wings: With two wings they covered their faces, with two they covered their feet, and with two they were flying. ³ And they were calling to one another: "Holy, holy, holy is the Lord Almighty;* **the whole earth is full of his glory**.*"* (Isaiah 6:1-3 - NIV - Emphasis Added)

As we pray from a position of Throne Room principles, we insist that the nations comply with the terms and conditions of the Word of God. It is from this place that we demand ownership of its resources and declare war on those who rebel against the will of the Father.

Prayer must be wrought for the pleasure of ownership and the correct use of all things.

b) **God's Throne Is the Most Exalted Throne in The Universe. There Is No Other Ruler, Throne or Kingdom Greater Than His.**

⁸ In the year that King Uzziah died, I saw the Lord **seated on a throne, high and exalted**. (Isaiah 6:8 - NIV - Emphasis Added)

³⁴ At the end of that time, I, Nebuchadnezzar, raised my eyes toward heaven, and my sanity was restored. Then I praised the Most High; I honored and glorified him who lives forever. **His dominion is an eternal dominion; his kingdom endures from generation to generation.** *35 All the peoples of the earth are regarded as nothing. He does as he pleases with the powers of heaven and the peoples of the earth. No one can hold back his hand or say to him: "What have you done?"* (Daniel 4:34-35 - NIV - Emphasis Added)

Note in the passage above that there is a level of insanity that can affect leaders. Nebuchadnezzar's sanity came back to him when he acknowledged that the Most High rules over all, and that His Kingdom is above all other kingdoms.

Prayer from the Throne, places us in a position to ensure the coronation of the Lord Jesus within the four corners of the earth. The culture of the Kingdom of God is in radical opposition to those in the world. The kingdoms of this world **must** become the Kingdom of our God and of His Christ.

¹⁵ And the seventh angel sounded; and there were great voices in heaven, saying, **The kingdoms of this world are become the kingdoms of our Lord, and of his Christ; and he shall reign for ever and ever**. (Revelation 11:15 - KJV - Emphasis Added)

This is what advanced level intercession entails. We are to spiritually attack every political system in the world through prayer. Many of them are based on bad, unjust and sometimes even wicked philosophies. Even the best of them are established around evil ideologies. Communism, Socialism, Feudalism, Democracy or Monarchy, all of them come up short when measured against the Kingdom of God. His Kingdom and His Throne are above all else. It is through our strategic intercession that we change Governments and rulers.

c) **God's Throne Is Eternal. There Can Never Be an Overthrow.**

⁷ **The Lord reigns forever**; *he has established his throne for judgment.* (Psalm 9:7 - NIV - Emphasis Added)

It is our understanding that the rulers of the world want to get rid of the Lord Jesus and all that He stands for. Throughout history, they murdered His prophets and enslaved His people. They burnt thousands of Bibles; closed institutions of learning and created ungodly laws. They threw prayer out of schools and removed biblical studies from curriculums.

¹ Why do the nations conspire and the peoples plot in vain? ² The kings of the earth rise up and the rulers band together against the Lord and against his anointed, saying, ³ "Let us break their chains and throw off their shackles." (Psalm 2:1-3 - NIV)

d) **His Throne Is the Capital of The Universe and The Administrative Center of His Kingdom.**

⁷⁻⁸ But the Lord lives on forever; he sits upon his throne to judge justly the nations of the world. ⁹ All who are oppressed may come to him. He is a refuge for them in their times of trouble. (Psalm 9:8-9 - TLB)

⁸ God reigns over the nations; God is seated on his holy throne. ⁹ The nobles of the nations assemble as the people of the God of Abraham, for the kings of the earth belong to God; he is greatly exalted. (Psalm 47:8-9 - NIV)

e) God Rules in Righteousness

⁶ Your throne, O God, will last for ever and ever; a scepter of justice will be the scepter of your kingdom. ⁷ You love righteousness and hate wickedness; (Psalm 45:6-7a - NIV)

When we apply these principles to our prayers, we pray with authority against the forces of injustice and call upon the Lord to bring equity and balance and manifest His greatness against all forms of wickedness in the earth. God is a defender of the weak, the widows, the poor, the orphans and the disabled. When we pray at this level, we execute written judgements against wicked and unjust governmental systems.

In the USA, we have seen in recent years the proliferation of violence against people of color. I have seen where a man strapped a bomb on himself intending to blow up people in New York. The cops were able to disarm that situation and apprehend the criminal. In Canada, the cops caught a man suspected of mowing down several people on a sidewalk. He murdered some ten persons. When confronted by the cops, he had what could have been mistaken for a gun and he was aiming it at a cop. Yet they were able to defuse the situation, disarm him, and then apprehend him without shooting him. The misuse of power in killing so many innocent lives is shocking in our times. We are encouraged to execute a new wave of intercession against the brutal use of excessive force.

Prayer can change situations like these. Time would fail to tell of injustices dished out against immigrants from certain parts of the world, of unjust financial products, poor public policy regarding education and healthcare. Time would not permit us to talk about the inequitable distribution of the wealth of the world. Our revelation of the Throne of God will plunge us into levels of intercession to combat these sinister, unjust powers. These are the things that the Bible speaks of as "the weightier matters of the Law."

As we pray from the position of the Throne, we attack and destroy every unholy thing in the earth. We must rule from the place and position of righteousness in our own lives. When established in righteousness in a practical way—not as one receiving forgiveness every day for sins committed, but from our victorious place—we can confidently wage a good warfare against the enemy of our souls.

³ For though we live in the world, we do not wage war as the world does. ⁴ The weapons we fight with are not the weapons of the world. On the contrary, they have divine power to demolish strongholds. ⁵ We demolish arguments and every pretension that sets itself up against the knowledge of God, and we take captive every thought to make it obedient to Christ. ⁶ And we will be ready to punish every act of disobedience, once your obedience is complete. (2 Corinthians 10:3-6 - NIV)

We are only able to punish disobedience when our obedience is completely fulfilled in the earth, and in a practical manner. Although much is being said of God's grace towards man in this dispensation, we must be sure to include the relevance and power of **practical piety**. The weapons we fight with to destroy enemy strongholds must be used in the hands or the mouths of those who are *practically* righteous.

The prayer of a righteous man produces amazing results. James advocates this. His revelation of 'holiness' is not one of flippantly being granted righteousness as a free gift without righteous acts to back it up. James is talking about believing; and endorsing this belief with righteous living from the place of demonstrative and practical holiness. See the emphasis from several versions of the Bible:

¹⁶ *...The prayer of a righteous person is powerful and effective.* (James 5:16b - NIV)

¹⁶ *...The effectual fervent prayer of a righteous man availeth much.* (James 5:16b KJV)

¹⁶ *...The earnest (heartfelt, continued) prayer of a righteous man makes tremendous power available [dynamic in its working].* (James 5:16b - AMPC)

God looked for a man to save the cities of Sodom and Gomorrah (Genesis chapter 18). He found righteous Abraham, who was willing to intercede on behalf of the people of that land in order to avert judgement. Abraham pleaded with God to spare the doomed cities if He could find at least fifty righteous people there. God agreed. Considering that there may be less than fifty righteous in the land, Abraham pressed on in intercession, reducing the numbers several times until it came to a point where he advocated for ten righteous persons. Abraham stopped there and did not continue to bargain, certain, I'm sure, that ten was a safe number to stop at. He had reasoned with God to the end and each time God was willing to change His position to show mercy instead of judgement. Abraham was an intercessor 'par excellence'. Remember that God said for fifty He would not destroy the city. Yet Abraham got God to reduce this number five times. It is important to see how a righteous man entered this 'Throne Room Dimension' and participated in a divine initiative. Here, in prayer, we see a man ruling with God.

f) **Administrating in A Seated Position**

There is hardly any picture of God 'standing' in His administration of the Universe. He is viewed as being 'seated' on the Throne. This position signifies that:

a. There is no credible threat to His Sovereignty.

b. Everything God does is easy. Jeremiah proclaims this:

> ¹⁷ *"Ah, Sovereign Lord, you have made the heavens and the earth by your great power and outstretched arm.* **Nothing is too hard for you**. (Jeremiah 32:17 - NIV - Emphasis Added)

c. Everything that God plans to do must be regarded as done.

We will later see that this information serves to configure our prayers. We must pray from the place of finished realities. The intercessor must be one who completely trusts that the thing for which he is praying is done.

g) **His Throne Is the Seat of Mercy**

The Tabernacle of Moses is an amazing description of the design of the Throne of God. Moses was told to build it after the pattern in the heavenlies.

⁹ *Make this tabernacle and all its furnishings exactly like the pattern I will show you.* (Exodus 25:9 - NIV)

¹⁷ *"You shall make a **mercy seat** of pure gold; two and a half cubits shall be its length and a cubit and a half its width.* ¹⁸ *And you shall make two cherubim of gold; of hammered work you shall make them at the two ends of the mercy seat.* (Exodus 25:17-18 - NKJV)

⁴⁰ *See that you make them according to the pattern shown you on the mountain.* (Exodus 25:40 - NIV)

This 'Mercy Seat' is a type of the 'Throne of God'.

¹ *Now the main point of what we are saying is this: We do have such a high priest, who sat down at the right hand of the throne of the Majesty in heaven,* ²*and who serves in the sanctuary, the true tabernacle set up by the Lord, not by a mere human being.* (Hebrews 8:1-2 - NIV)

The incredible truth taught here is: that the foundational attitude of God towards mankind as He uses laws and justice, is 'mercy'. The constant revelation of God or of Christ seated on the Throne is the idea that God's policies are designed to do man **good** and not harm. It indicates that He does not want to dish out judgement upon man for sins committed. The entire administration of God and His

Kingdom is one of immense goodwill and patience toward mankind. It is from this place, 'Throne Room Prayer' is built. No matter how deep in sin man may fall, we are to pray for the lifting up of man at the 'Mercy Seat', and not for his utter destruction. Imprecatory prayers, pronouncing curses of doom on others, is not the befitting thing for a believer to do. Even in wrath, God remembers to be merciful.

This new dimension of prayer of which we speak is based upon the reality of the existence of a Mercy Seat. We are to call upon the Lord for the salvation of villages, towns and cities. Prayers that are prayed from the Throne are designed to create revival and reformation. They will bring about national healing, peace and prosperity. Often, we curse Governments and insult its leaders. In the state of displeasure over the debauchery we often see, we tend to switch on carnal desires and pray for their ruin. However, when we see the Lord on His Throne of Mercy, we see His love and care for the peoples of the world, no matter their condition.

h) **The Throne Is A Spiritual Position of Authority**

The Old Testament has phenomenal truths hidden in its emblems and artifacts, in its numbers, colors, feast days and festive times.

Great truths could be found in its priesthood, tabernacle and protocols. In theological circles, it is said that, "The Old Testament is the New Testament concealed; and the New Testament is the Old Testament revealed."

[16] Therefore do not let anyone judge you by what you eat or drink, or with regard to a religious festival, a New Moon celebration or a Sabbath day. [17] These are a **shadow** *of the things that were to come; the reality, however, is found in Christ.* (Colossians 2:16-18 - NIV)

We, then, should establish that the idea of the 'Throne of God' has more to do with the highest levels of 'privilege' and 'authority' in the Universe, rather than an antique chair to sit on. The term 'throne' has great power when it comes to defining 'spiritual authority'. Additional words that can be applied in relation to the Throne are 'Reign', 'Kings and Queens', 'Rulers', and 'Sovereignty'. These words describe both the authority of God and that of His people in the earth.

I will continue to develop the glory of this concept as it relates to a praying Church. We are a people of authority, and so, sit on thrones.

Seated on Your Throne

The Body of Christ is also Seated with Christ in Heavenly Places

Among other things, redemption deals with the identifying of the believer with the Lord. We were buried with Him in baptism, rose with Him in the resurrection, and shall sit with Him in the heavenlies as well. It is, then, safe to say that we are seated with the Lord on the Throne. In this regard, we are to share His authority in the world.

> *⁴ But because of his great love for us, God, who is rich in mercy, ⁵ made us alive with Christ even when we were dead in transgressions—it is by grace you have been saved.* **⁶ And God raised us up with Christ and seated us with him in the heavenly realms in Christ Jesus,** *⁷ in order that in the coming ages he might show the incomparable riches of his grace, expressed in his kindness to us in Christ Jesus. ⁸ For it is by grace you have been saved, through faith—and this is not from yourselves, it is the gift of God—* (Ephesians 2:4-8 - NIV - Emphasis Added)

John the Apostle, who probably had the most consistent and vivid picture of the Church in its exalted place, saw other thrones around the Throne of God. Consider the following passages:

> *² At once I was in the Spirit, and there before me was a throne in heaven with someone sitting on it. ³ And the one who sat there had the appearance of jasper and ruby. A rainbow, resembling an emerald, encircled the throne.* **⁴ Surrounding the throne were twenty-four other thrones, and seated on them were twenty-four elders.** *They were dressed in white and had crowns of gold on their heads. ⁵ From the throne came flashes of lightning, rumblings and peals*

of thunder. In front of the throne, seven lamps were blazing. These are the seven spirits of God. ⁶ *Also in front of the throne there was what looked like a sea of glass, clear as crystal...* (Revelation 4:2-6a - NIV - Emphasis Added)

¹⁶ *And the twenty-four elders,* **who were seated on their thrones before God,** *fell on their faces and worshiped God,* ¹⁷ *saying: "We give thanks to you, Lord God Almighty, the One who is and who was, because you have taken your great power and have begun to reign.* (Revelation 11:16-17 - NIV - Emphasis Added)

We tippy-toe through the grass here. The imagery is stunning, to say the least. God's Throne is seen as being surrounded by other thrones, according to Revelation 4:4. It is important to see that God's Throne is not one big chair that had space for all the other people seated. Rather, each person had his own throne. The thrones were positioned *around* the Throne of God. They were facing God. It is clear that they faced Him without condemnation and fear. In his vision, John noted the majestic look of unapproachable light, universal responsibility (peals of lightning and thunder), beauty, and excellence.

Those seated around the Throne are the redeemed—those who are seated in heavenly places *in* Christ Jesus. Each member of the Body of Christ is charged with executing the universal, timeless, plans of God. We are to share with Christ, the management of the material world, enforcement of the principles of God, and judgement of demons. Such should

be our prayers. We must pray with this abiding awareness. We are not beggars and paupers; No! We are not lambs to the slaughter; No! **We are more than conquerors!** Our Father has given us a place in His Kingdom in which we participate in His plans and promises.

Revelation 20:4-6 confirms it this way:

> *⁴ I saw thrones on which were seated those who had been given authority to judge. And I saw the souls of those who had been beheaded because of their testimony about Jesus and because of the word of God. They had not worshiped the beast or its image and had not received its mark on their foreheads or their hands. They came to life and reigned with Christ a thousand years. ⁵ (The rest of the dead did not come to life until the thousand years were ended.) This is the first resurrection. ⁶ Blessed and holy are those who share in the first resurrection. The second death has no power over them, but they will be priests of God and of Christ and will reign with him for a thousand years.* (Revelation 20:4-6 - NIV)

Appointed to the World's Tribunal

The Throne is a place where justice in a nation is executed. If the Church is clearly seated in the heavenly realms with God in the place of His Throne, it is irrefutable that this is the setting of a Tribunal. A 'Tribunal' is a group of magistrates seated on an elevated place for the administration of justice. The origin of the word speaks to the order of managing the affairs of a tribe. This picture is of the Church congregating with the Father in His administration of justice over the nations. The Church is in the world's tribunal. Another way of saying this, is that we have been elected as the 'Supreme Court of the Universe'.

i) **Prophetic Declarations of The World's Tribunal:** It appears that David the King had some insights to this reality when he wrote the 149th Psalm.

> *⁵ Let the saints be joyful in glory; Let them sing aloud on their beds. ⁶ Let the high praises of God be in their mouth, And a two-edged sword in their hand, ⁷ To execute vengeance on the nations, And punishments on the peoples; ⁸ To bind their kings with chains, And their nobles with fetters of iron; ⁹ To execute on them the written judgment—This honor have all His saints.* (Psalm 149:5-9 - NKJV)

In this Psalm, David presents an unusual picture of God's people as if functioning in a 'Tribunal' with God. His reference is to Zion as 'the people of God', and calls them in verse five, 'the saints of God'. The actions mentioned after, speak of jurisprudence. These 'saints' have a 'double-edged sword' in their hands. This refers to the authority of the Word of God in fighting mode. The text goes on to say that the saints of God are to inflict vengeance upon nations. He references here:

ungodly cultures; secular spheres where Christ is not acknowledged as Lord and God's Word is not the final authority on matters of faith and behavior.

The passage here also deals with inflicting punishment upon the heathen peoples of the earth. The idea here is to cause their plans and efforts which have been prepared without God, to crumble and fall until they turn to the Lord. Then it speaks of binding their nobles with fetters of iron, meaning: to set prohibitions around their administration and political agendas. This 'saintly' Tribunal is to ensure that the Kingdom of God is enforced upon the earth. Through our prayers, we are to control the worldly governmental systems. Then, finally, David points out the fact that this 'Tribunal' is to carry out the sentences or judgements written against tribes and towns, to bring them into obedience of God.

ii) **Hall of Justice Shaped Like the Chambers of The Bride.** When Solomon designed the Throne of Israel, it was positioned in the Hall of Justice. It was from this place that his wisdom was disseminated across the nation for the good of all Israel.

^{7} He built the throne hall, the Hall of Justice, where he was to judge, and he covered it with cedar from floor

to ceiling. ⁸ *And the palace in which he was to live, set farther back, was similar in design. Solomon also made a palace like this hall for Pharaoh's daughter, whom he had married.* (1 Kings 7:7-8 - NIV)

What is striking here is that he also designed his palace like the Hall of Justice. Furthermore, the palace and chambers where his wife, the daughter of Pharaoh of all persons, lived, was designed in similar fashion to the Hall of Justice. By this we can see—in a prototypical way—God's intentions for the Chambers of the Bride of Christ to be designed with the same functionality as the Hall of Justice. It is as if the President of the United States designed the home of the First Lady, exactly like the White House.

The Chambers of the Bride, then, is intended to function in the same way as the Hall of Justice. I think that this is a remarkable truth, and it is even more astounding when this truth is applied. Of all the wives, the daughter of one of Israel's greatest arch-enemies—Pharaoh—was given this honor. How much more should we, who are called the 'Bride of Christ'?

⁶ *Then I heard what sounded like a great multitude, like the roar of rushing waters and like loud peals of thunder, shouting: "Hallelujah! For our Lord God Almighty reigns.* ⁷ *Let us rejoice and be glad and give*

him glory! **For the wedding of the Lamb has come,** *and* **his bride has made herself ready.** ⁸ *Fine linen, bright and clean, was given her to wear." (Fine linen stands for the righteous acts of the saints.)* (Revelation 19:6-8 - NIV)

The voice came from the Throne saying that, **"The Bride is ready!"** This sends chills down my spine. The Bride is not necessarily ready for fleshly intimacy, but in this spiritual dimension, she is finally ready to take her place in the Universe, sitting in the chambers with the Bridegroom, making decisions concerning the destiny of the nations.

The context of this 'royal wedding' is the 'Throne Room of God', and it clearly refers to the 'Reign of the Lord Almighty'. The Bride enters into this dimension to rule and reign with the Lord. This is the honor of all the saints. This is the level of intercession to which the saints are called.

The book of Revelation does two main things for us. Firstly, it is the unveiling of the person of Christ in His divine nature and purposes. Then it demonstrates the original design and the intent of God in history, to call forth a people unto Himself to share in the governance of the nations of the earth with His Son. The Church is an eternal companion for the Lamb of God—Jesus, the Christ.

In a sense, God is repeating the Genesis charge here. When He gave Adam the Universe to manage, He said, "It is not good for the man to be alone." Another way of putting this is: "It is not good for the man to manage the world all by himself." God's solution was to make Adam a bride, or a wife. In the same way, we are seeing that the world was made by Christ, and for Him. He is the only begotten of the Father. It would be easy to visualize God, in His musings, saying, "It is not good for Christ to be alone. It is not good for Him to own and manage the world by Himself. I would make Him a wife." So, the Father made use of thousands of years, and finally produced a 'Bride' suitable for His Son. *"The Bride of Christ is ready!"*

The World Tomorrow – New World Order

It is almost impossible to describe this subject in all its fullness; and again, we must move with bated breath and tippy-toe through the grass when we enter this domain. It is the cataclysmic end of the world as we know it. Revelation chapter twenty-one is describing the final picture of redeemed humanity in perfect union with Christ. One's heart would read this passage and weep in incredible awe and unspeakable joy.

> [9] One of the seven angels who had the seven bowls full of the seven last plagues came and said to me, "Come, I will show you the bride, the wife of the Lamb." [10] And he carried me away in the Spirit to a mountain great and high, and showed me the Holy City, Jerusalem, coming down out of heaven from God. [11] It shone with the glory of God, and its

brilliance was like that of a very precious jewel, like a jasper, clear as crystal. ¹² It had a great, high wall with twelve gates, and with twelve angels at the gates. On the gates were written the names of the twelve tribes of Israel. ¹³ There were three gates on the east, three on the north, three on the south and three on the west. ¹⁴ The wall of the city had twelve foundations, and on them were the names of the twelve apostles of the Lamb. (Revelation 21:9-14 - NIV)

The passage speaks of the world tomorrow. This truly is the 'New World Order'. Many ungodly institutions and men of power, wealth, and renown are planning to bring in an order of human culture where Christ does not reign. But God will laugh at their calamity. The 'New World' is one where Christ Jesus is the King of Kings and the Lord of Lords. It is one where all the sectors of human society are administered according to divine jurisprudence. It is the order where, not just the earth, but every demon spirit, galaxies and regions light years away, are ruled by Christ and His Bride—the Church.

The Apostle Paul ends his description of the power of God in Ephesians by referring to this world.

²⁰ Now unto him that is able to do exceeding abundantly above all that we ask or think, according to the power that worketh in us, ²¹ Unto him be glory in the church by Christ Jesus throughout all ages, **world without end.** *Amen.* (Ephesians 3:20-21 - KJV - Emphasis Added)

He calls it the "world without end." *The Message* version of the Bible points to this more graphically.

> *²⁰ God can do anything, you know—far more than you could ever imagine or guess or request in your wildest dreams! He does it not by pushing us around but by working within us, his Spirit deeply and gently within us. ²¹ Glory to God in the church! Glory to God in the Messiah, in Jesus! Glory down all the generations! Glory through all millennia! Oh, yes!* (Ephesians 3:20-21 - MSG)

Furthermore, the writer of the book of Hebrews speaks to the issue in this way:

> *⁵ And have tasted the good word of God, and* **the powers of the world to come,** (Hebrews 6:5 - KJV - Emphasis Added)

This is where we speak of the Kingdom that is now, and not yet. Everything that the Kingdom will be, can be experienced now. The Church will reign with the Lord in the world to come. As far as God is concerned, at our born again experience we entered into that dimension.

We have taken time to establish the theological foundation upon which we should base our desires and prayers. We are not saying that we should not cast our cares upon the Lord or pray for the mundane; we are saying that there is a new level of prayer to which the Church is called. This level finds its context in the ultimate intention of God for His people. Our subject matters must be derived from the heart of the Father.

Of significant importance, is the matter of jurisprudence, justice and fairness for all the peoples of the world. The Church's role in prayer must be to engage Heaven to bring equality and balance within the world. Prayer must be the enforcement of justice of God in the earth. This is why much of Paul's writings point to the Church's role in deciding matters that ensure justice.

1. **The Saints Should Not Go Before an Earthly Judicial System**

   ¹ If any of you has a dispute against another, how dare you take it to court before the unrighteous, and not before the saints? (1 Corinthians 6:1 - CSB)

   ⁵ I say this to shame you. Is it possible that there is nobody among you wise enough to judge a dispute between believers? ⁶ But instead, one brother takes another to court—and this in front of unbelievers! (1 Corinthians 6:5-6 - NIV)

2. **The Saints Shall Judge the World**

   ² Do you not know that **the saints will judge the world?** *And if the world will be judged by you, are you unworthy to judge the smallest matters?* (1 Corinthians 6:2 - NKJV)

3. **The Saints Shall Sit in Judgement Over the Angels**

   ³ Do you not know also that we [Christians] are **to judge the [very] angels** *and pronounce opinion* between right and wrong [for them]? How much more then [as to] matters pertaining to this world and of this life only! (1 Corinthians 6:3 - AMPC)

4. **The Saints Have to Authority to Forgive Sins**

   ²¹ Again Jesus said, "Peace be with you! As the Father has sent me, I am sending you." ²² And with that he breathed on them and said, "Receive the Holy Spirit. **²³ If you forgive anyone's sins, their sins are forgiven; if you do not forgive them, they are not forgiven."** (John 20:21-23 - NIV)

5. **The Saints Have the Authority to Banish A Person from The Kingdom of God.**

   ⁴ When you are assembled in the name of our Lord Jesus, and I am with you in spirit, with the power of our Lord Jesus, ⁵ hand that one over to Satan for the destruction of the flesh, so that his spirit may be saved in the day of the Lord. (1 Corinthians 5:4-5 - CSB)

It cannot be denied: The Church has been ordained by God to judge matters of great importance. The word used for 'judge' in these cases is a Greek word 'Krino' [pronounced 'kre'-no']. It means to decide on a matter with regards to what and who is right, good or bad, and to issue a decree of condemnation on the bad and blessing upon the good. This level of judicial administration is usually carried out within a Tribunal System. Hence, Paul teaches that we (corporately) can deliver a man over to Satan. When he spoke of this, he set the criteria for judging troublesome situations within the Church. In essence, he was saying that, "When you are gathered, and the blessing of Senior Leadership is present and in agreement, and the presence and the power of Christ the great Judge is there, then you can give a corporate judgement on the matter and declare the outcome."

We cannot dance around this matter. It is clear to see that this has always been the design of God. Righteous humanity is given power beyond what we have commonly known. Our prayers should be operating in this realm. We must come off the floor level of simply begging God for things, because we have access to an abundance of things. The mere fact that we are in the Kingdom of God means that we have been given authority to rule over the world.

Dear Reader, let these words inspire you to activate your faith. Let them provoke a new passion for Prayer. Let them build in you a new vocabulary and fresh sense of passion to talk with God. As a member of the 'World's Supreme Court' and 'Tribunal', God respects your requests and your opinions. Your righteous perspectives are considered when God decides on a matter. Arise from your state of spiritual slumber and prayerlessness and push your way into the deep things of God. Pray from your position on the Throne. Ask for the nations; for cities, towns and villages. Let me echo our Lord's glorious promise on this:

> *[7] Let me tell you what God said next. He said, "You're my son, And today is your birthday. [8] What do you want? Name it: Nations as a present? continents as a prize? [9] You can command them all to dance for you,*

Or throw them out with tomorrow's trash. (Psalm 2:7-9 - MSG).

May we unite in our understanding of who we are and what God purposed from the beginning of time. May we come to know the riches of our inheritance with the saints in light, and may we come to know the all-surpassing power of God that is in us.

Take your place around the Throne and pray like a king. Pray like you are an authentic child of God. Pray with a new level of confidence. Pray from the place of finished realities and as if you are the owner of all things. I believe these truths, if applied, would bring incredible results and raise up a new breed of intercessors to the glory of God.

Prayer

Sovereign Lord, I stand amazed at your perfection and your greatness. You made all the world through the power of your Word, and uphold all things through the same words you spoke. You are omnipotent.

You have chosen us to sit with you in the Throne Room of Heaven and given us to share in the administration of the world. Fill me with wisdom, knowledge, discretion and understanding. Make me to know proverbs, maxims, parables and riddles. Help me to have a clear and precise understanding of the mysteries of God that I may execute your purposes with authority and righteousness.

I commit to pray over kings and governmental systems that the salvation of God may overtake nations. I pray for them, that they would govern with justice and wisdom, and in a way that the peoples of my nation would live in unity and harmony. I dismantle and destroy every dark force interfering with their hearts, and declare the Congress, the Judiciary, and the executive branches of Government are run in the fear of God and honor for all its peoples, in the mighty name of Jesus!

NOTES

NOTES

NOTES

NOTES

NOTES

NOTES

More Great Resources From Dr. Peter Bonadie Ministries

Books:
- Understanding The Kingdom
- Curses, Causes and Cures
- Seven Manifestations of the Curse
- You Can Make Dry Bones Live
- Kingdom of gods

Contact Information:

DR. PETER BONADIE MINISTRIES
770 Park Place
Brooklyn, New York 11216
Phone: 1.888.643.4442
Email: apostlebonadie@gmail.com
www.peterbonadieministries.org